The Middle-earth Quiz Book

The Middle-earth Quiz Book

SUZANNE BUCHHOLZ

Houghton Mifflin Company Boston
1979

Copyright © 1979 by Patricia Suzanne Buchholz

All rights reserved. No part of this work may be reproduced or transmitted in any form by any means, electronic or mechanical, including photocopying and recording, or by any information storage or retrieval system, without permission in writing from the publisher.

Library of Congress Cataloging in Publication Data

Buchholz, Suzanne.
  The Middle-earth quiz book.

  1. Tolkien, John Ronald Reuel, 1892–1973—Miscellanea. 2. Tolkien, John Ronald Reuel, 1892–1973. Hobbit. 3. Tolkien, John Ronald Reuel, 1892–1973. Lord of the rings. 4. Tolkien, John Ronald Reuel, 1892–1973. Silmarillion. I. Title.
PR6039.032Z59   823'.9'12   79-9469
ISBN 0-395-28428-7 pbk.

Printed in the United States of America

U 10 9 8 7 6 5 4 3 2 1

DEDICATED TO

Daddy — who always knew I could,
Mom — who could read my handwriting,
and
Larry — for being there

CONTENTS

Introduction xi

	Questions	Answers

The Hobbit

QUESTIONS

	Questions	Answers
1. "His Name Was Baggins"	3	93
2. "Far Over the Misty Mountains Grim"	4	94
3. "The Mountain Smoked Beneath the Moon"	5	95
4. "To Dungeons Deep and Caverns Old"	6	96

QUOTATIONS

1. "Cheat the Goblins of Their Sport!"	7	96
2. "Something Strange Is Happening"	8	97

TRIVIA

1. "Lazy Lob and Crazy Cob"	9	97

The Fellowship of the Ring

QUESTIONS

1. "The One Ring to Rule Them All"	10	98
2. "But What About This Frodo?"	11	99
3. "Well, Now We're Off at Last!"	12	99
4. "There's Something Funny about All This"	13	100

CONTENTS		vii
	Questions	*Answers*
5. "There Were Mysterious Wanderers"	14	100
6. "Down into the Land of Shadow"	15	101
QUOTATIONS		
1. "Servant of the Secret Fire"	16	101
2. "You . . . You're a Brandybuck!"	17	102
3. "Power of the Dark Lord!"	18	102
TRIVIA		
1. "The World Was Fair"	19	103
2. "The Mountains Tall"	20	103

The Two Towers

QUESTIONS		
1. "The Orcs Were Getting Ready"	21	104
2. "The King of the Golden Hall"	22	104
3. Flotsam and Jetsam	23	105
4. Past the Marshes, Beyond the Black Gate	24	105
5. "An Evil Thing in Spider-form"	25	106
QUOTATIONS		
1. "There Is Evil Afoot"	26	106
2. "An Old Liar with Honey on His Forked Tongue?"	27	107
TRIVIA		
1. "The Window on the West"	28	107
2. Perils of the Journey	29	108

The Return of the King

QUESTIONS		
1. "Seven Stars, Seven Stones, One White Tree"	30	109
2. "Ride Now, Ride Now! Ride to Gondor!"	31	109
3. "Lord of the Black Land Come Forth!"	32	110

	Questions	Answers
4. "War Now Calls Us!"	33	110
5. "Towers Strong and High"	34	111
6. "The Crack of Doom"	35	111
7. "The Ring-bearer Has Fulfilled His Quest"	36	112
8. Partings	37	112
9. Trouble at the Shire	38	113
10. "The End of Fellowship in the Middle-earth"	38	113

QUOTATIONS

	Questions	Answers
1. "We Must Ride Our Own Road"	39	114
2. "The Houses of Lamentation"	40	114
3. "A Piece of Elvish Glass"	41	115
4. "Go in Peace!"	42	115

TRIVIA

	Questions	Answers
1. The Sounds of War	43	116
2. Who and What	44	116

APPENDICES

	Questions	Answers
A–I. Kingdoms of the Middle-earth	45	117
A–II. Notes from a Loremaster's Journal	46	117
A–III. Who, What, and When	47	118
B. Legends of the Ages	48	118

The Silmarillion

QUESTIONS

	Questions	Answers
1. "The Beginning of Days"	49	119
2. "The Darkening"	49	119
3. Lore of the Ancients	50	120
4. "The Hidden King"	50	120
5. "Tales of Sorrow"	51	121
6. "The Doom Lies in Yourself"	51	121
7. Elves and Men	52	122
8. The War of Wrath	52	122

CONTENTS		
	Questions	Answers
TRIVIA		
1. Elves, Dwarves, and Balrogs	53	123
AKALLABÊTH	53	123

People — Fair Friends and Fierce Foes

	Questions	Answers
1. Aragorn	54	124
2. Bilbo Baggins	54	124
3. Bilbo's Birthday	55	125
4. Tom Bombadil	55	125
5. Fair Friends of Fierce Foes	56	126
6. Dwarves	57	126
7. More Dwarves	57	127
8. Elves	58	127
9. More Elves	59	128
10. Ents	60	128
11. Gandalf the Grey	60	129
12. Gollum	61	129
13. Hobbits	62	130
14. More Hobbits	63	130
15. Famous Hobbits	64	131
16. Names	64	131
17. More Names	65	132
18. The Nazgûl	66	132
19. Sauron	66	133
20. Spouses	67	133
21. Types of Peoples	68	134
22. The Valar	69	134
23. More on the Valar	70	135

Places

	Questions	Answers
1. Inns	71	136
2. Forests	72	136
3. Moria	73	137
4. Mountains and Hills	74	137
5. Rivers	75	138
6. Towers	75	138

	Questions	Answers

Others

	Questions	Answers
1. Animals	76	139
2. More Animals	76	139
3. Battle Quiz	77	140
4. More Battles	78	140
5. Emblems	79	141
6. Horses	80	141
7. Middle-earth Match-up	81	142
8. More Match-ups	82	142
9. Miscellaneous Match-up	83	143
10. The Palantíri	84	143
11. The Riddle Game	85	144
12. The Rings	86	144
13. More on the Rings	87	145
14. Weapons	88	145
15. Trees	89	146
16. Who Killed _____ ?	89	146

INTRODUCTION

I wrote this quiz book out of my love for J. R. R. Tolkien's Middle-earth. I am fascinated by his creation of an entire world with its many peoples, history, and geography. I found that writing these quizzes helped me pay more attention to his books, to remember facts and understand them more easily. I hope answering these quizzes will do the same for you.

They were written to test your recollection of the creatures, objects, and events portrayed in Tolkien's *The Hobbit, The Lord of the Rings,* and *The Silmarillion.* Perhaps when you are looking up the answers to these questions you will find yourself rereading sections of the books, reliving your favorite episodes or discovering new passages you may have overlooked.

You can test your knowledge alone on a bleak and lonely Sunday, engulfing yourself in the perils of Middle-earth. You and a friend can challenge each other to see who can come up with the most right answers. Or you can use these quizzes as a catalyst for group discussion (or argument).

This book is made up of 101 quizzes with approximately ten questions each. The majority of the questions are simple to answer. Most can be dealt with in a few words or less although some will need a more detailed answer. I've tried to make the questions as clear as possible, which may make some seem a little long-winded.

Twelve of the quizzes are matching. In these you match the name or word in the first column with its description or definition in the second column. The three Miscellaneous quizzes are ones in which you match an object such as athelas with its definition (I'm not going to give you the answer!). Or, for another example, in

More Names you match the person's name—such as Aragorn—with the one or more other names he went by. In More Battles you match the name of the battle with the two warring factions. The matching quizzes are somewhat easier because you are given all the answers. (You just have to recognize them.)

There is one chronology quiz. In the Battles quiz I list seventeen battles from the First Age through the Third Age. You are supposed to arrange them in the order in which they were fought. It's a difficult quiz and you deserve a pat on the back if you get them correct. (Don't overdo it though!).

The book is divided into eight sections. There are five book sections—one each on *The Hobbit,* The *Fellowship of the Ring,* The *Two Towers, The Return of the King,* and *The Silmarillion,* plus sections on People, Places, and Others. Others is a catch-all classification for all the quizzes that didn't fit any other category.

The sections on each of the five books are, for the most part, written in the order in which they are read. I did it this way to make it easier for you to look up the answers. This way you will know that the answers to Quiz 8 in *The Return of the King* will be found nearer the end of the book than the answers to Quiz 5. The exceptions to this are found in *The Hobbit* and *The Fellowship of the Ring* sections. The first Questions quiz and the first Quotations quiz in these sections span the whole book.

The People, Places, and Others sections cover all five books. The answers to each quiz will come from more than one book. This will make the answers to these quizzes more difficult to look up than those in the book sections. (You'll just have to reread all the books.) The indexes in the back of *The Return of the King* and *The Silmarillion* may help you with these quizzes.

You may feel that the people and places contained in the books are not evenly represented in these sections, but I found that some of the people and places had been thoroughly covered in the five book sections. I didn't want to repeat the same material. Frodo Baggins is a perfect example. Certainly as a major character he deserved a separate quiz. But since all of *The Lord of the Rings* is his story he was already the subject of many questions. A separate quiz seemed repetitious. The same reasoning applied to Rivendell and Lórien. You may not agree with me but that is how I decided.

Each of the five book sections is divided into three subsections—Questions, Quotations, and Trivia. I tried to vary the questions, making some of them easy enough for a first-time reader to answer while still challenging the many-times reader. You will notice there are more Questions quizzes in *The Return of the King* than in any of the other four book sections. *The Return of the King* is the culmination of *The Lord of the Rings* and *The Hobbit.* It is full of important events and major changes. I felt these questions would help you remember them all. (It helped me.)

The object of the Quotations quizzes is to identify the speaker, and where and to whom the quotation was made. The number of Quotations quizzes in each book depended on the amount of dialogue in it. *The Silmarillion* doesn't have a Quotations section because the dialogue in it was either too easy to identify or too hard to use as a question. Some of the quotations are trickier than they look so think carefully before you answer.

The Trivia quizzes are meant for the Tolkien experts. They test your attention to detail. For instance, the answer to one of these questions may be a single phrase buried in a lengthy paragraph. (Good luck!)

Well, I'll let you get started now. I hope you enjoy answering these quizzes as much as I enjoyed writing them.

SUZANNE

Questions

QUESTIONS

1. "His Name Was Baggins"

1. Name the thirteen Dwarves that Bilbo Baggins accompanied on their adventure to Erebor.
2. Who were the three Trolls the company first ran into and what did they do to the Dwarves?
3. What are moon-letters?
4. When is Durin's Day?
5. Who rescued the company from the Wargs?
6. What was the name of the skin-changer and what did he change into?
7. Gandalf didn't make the entire journey to Erebor with Thorin and Company. Where did he leave them?
8. All the Dwarves but Thorin were captured by the great spiders of Mirkwood. What happened to him?
9. What happened when Bombur fell into the water of the stream in Mirkwood?
10. Upon first encountering the dragon hoard, what did Bilbo take to prove to the Dwarves that he really was a burglar?

2. "Far Over the Misty Mountains Grim"

1. Why did Thorin and Company stop at Bilbo Baggins' home?
2. Why did Bilbo leave for his adventure without a hat, walking stick, or even a pocket-handkerchief?
3. What happens to Trolls if they are aboveground at dawn?
4. Where did Gandalf and Thorin get their swords and Bilbo his long knife?
5. Thorin and Company took refuge from a fierce storm in a cave on the Misty Mountains. What happened there?
6. When did the Dwarves first decide that Bilbo was a first-rate burglar after all?
7. Thorin and Company stumbled onto the meeting-place of the Wargs. What did Gandalf hear them planning?
8. Thorin and Company lost all their baggage and their ponies to the Goblins. Where did they get new supplies?
9. Why did the Company stray from the path through Mirkwood?
10. How did the Company escape from the Wood-elves?

3. "The Mountain Smoked Beneath the Moon"

1. What did the Goblins do when they came to meet the Wargs and saw Wargs and forest on fire and Thorin's Company in the trees?
2. Beorn, the skin-changer, didn't take kindly to strangers. How did Gandalf get him to accept their company of fifteen?
3. Beorn warned them of two things they must not do while in Mirkwood Forest. What were they?
4. The days in Mirkwood Forest were dark and dreary but the nights were worse because of what they saw. What did they see at night?
5. The moon-letters on Thorin's map tell how to find the key-hole to the secret entrance to Lonely Mountain. How?
6. Who was it that first noticed these moon-letters?
7. How did Bard know where to shoot the arrow that killed Smaug?
8. How much of a share of the dragon-hoard was claimed by Bard, as dragon-slayer and heir of Dale?
9. What was it that Bilbo gave Bard so that he might be able to bargain with Thorin?
10. What happened that caused the battle between the Dwarves, and the Elves and Men to be halted before it started?

4. "To Dungeons Deep and Caverns Old"

1. Who lived in a great cave within the eastern edge of Mirkwood?
2. Who was the first to see the Eagles coming to the Battle of the Five Armies?
3. Why couldn't Bilbo be found after the battle was ended?
4. In the last hour of the battle who came to the aid of the Elves, Dwarves, Men, and Eagles and how did he seem?
5. When Thorin was buried, what was buried with him?
6. As they parted company at the edge of Mirkwood, Bilbo gave the Elvenking a necklace of silver and pearls. Why?
7. After battling the spiders, the Dwarves and Bilbo made one last effort to find their way out of Mirkwood. Why didn't they make it?
8. What did Thorin give Bilbo when they first reached the dragon-hoard?
9. Who did Thorin send for to help protect the dragon-hoard from the Men?
10. How did he get in touch with him?

QUOTATIONS

1. "Cheat the Goblins of Their Sport!"

Who said the following and on what occasion:

1. "Now I know what a piece of bacon feels like when it is suddenly picked out of the pan on a fork and put back on the shelf!"
2. "What's a burrahobbit got to do with my pocket, anyways?"
3. "No! We are glad to cheat the goblins of their sport, and glad to repay our thanks to you, but we will not risk ourselves for dwarves in the southward plains."
4. "Well, it is the first time that even a mouse has crept along carefully and quietly under my very nose and not been spotted."
5. "It was a sharp struggle, but worth it. What nasty thick skins they have to be sure, but I'll wager there is good juice inside."
6. "Black Arrow! I have saved you to the last. You have never failed me and always I have recovered you. I had you from my father and he from of old. If ever you come from the forges of the true king under the Mountain, go now and speed well!"
7. "Up to no good, I'll warrant! Spying on the private business of my people, I guess! Thieves, I shouldn't be surprised to learn! Murderers and friends of Elves, not unlikely!"
8. "By the beard of Durin! I wish I had Gandalf here! Curse him for his choice of you! May his beard wither! As for you I will throw you to the rocks!"
9. "Lazy Lob and Crazy Cob
are weaving webs to wind me.
I am far more sweet than other meat,
but still they cannot find me!"
10. "We are worn and famished after our long road and we have sick comrades. Now make haste and let us have no more words or your master may have something to say to you."

2. "Something Strange Is Happening"

1. "We are plain quiet folk and have no use for adventures. Nasty disturbing uncomfortable things! Make you late for dinner!"

2. "You would have dropped him if a goblin had suddenly grabbed your leg from behind in the dark, tripped up your feet, and kicked you in the back!"

3. "A very good tale! The best I have heard for a long while. If all beggars could tell such a good one, they might find me kinder."

4. "No time now! You must follow me! We must all keep together and not risk getting separated. All of us must escape or none, and this is our last chance."

5. "Now come with me and taste the new wine that has just come in. I shall be hard at work clearing the cellars of the empty wood, so let us have a drink first to help the labour."

6. "To smell apples everlastingly when you can scarcely move and are cold and sick with hunger is maddening. I could eat anything in the wide world now, for hours on end—but not an apple!"

7. "I am too fat for such fly-walks. I should turn dizzy and tread on my beard, and then you would be thirteen again. And the knotted ropes are too slender for my weight."

8. "Something strange is happening. The time has gone for the autumn wanderings; and these are birds that dwell always in the land; there are starlings and flocks of finches; and far off there are many carrion birds as if a battle were afoot!"

9. "Since such is your answer, I declare the Mountain besieged. You shall not depart from it, until you call on your side for a truce and a parley. We will bear no weapons against you, but we leave you to your gold. You may eat that, if you will!"

10. "There is more in you of good than you know, child of the kindly West. Some courage and some wisdom, blended in measure. If more of us valued food and cheer and song above hoarded gold, it would be a merrier world."

TRIVIA

1. "Lazy Lob and Crazy Cob"

1. What did the wine of Dorwinion do to its drinkers?
2. What was the name of the butler to the King of the Wood-elves?
3. Before they learned to open the secret entrance to Lonely Mountain, Bilbo sat on its "doorstep" thinking and watching. What was he watching?
4. Under what sort of moon were the moon-letters on Thorin's map written?
5. In Smaug's dragon-hoard were spears made for King Bladorthin. What were they like?
6. What was the color of the cloak and hood given to Bilbo by Dwalin at the beginning of their journey?
7. In the Battle of the Five Armies, the banners of the Goblins were countless. What colors were they?
8. What month and day was it when Bilbo returned to Bag End?
9. What was it that Dáin restored to Bard, who in turn gave it to the Elvenking?
10. At Bilbo's house the Dwarves played music. What instrument did Thorin play?

QUESTIONS

1. "The One Ring to Rule Them All"

1. It is decided that the Ring must be destroyed. How?
2. A Fellowship is formed to aid Frodo on his Quest. Who are the eight other members?
3. What happened to Bilbo on his eleventy-first birthday?
4. During their last conversation in the Shire, Bilbo alarmed Gandalf by referring to the Ring as what?
5. Gandalf tells Frodo that it was no accident that Bilbo got the Ring from Gollum. What was the reason?
6. Why did Sam go on the Quest with Frodo?
7. Though no one else with him saw the Black Riders as anything but shadows, what did Frodo see at Weathertop and how did he come to see it?
8. In Khazad-dûm Frodo receives a fearful blow in the side from an Orkan spear. Why wasn't he killed by it?
9. What were the gifts Galadriel gave to Sam and Frodo on their departure from Lórien?
10. What happened to the Morgul-knife used to stab Frodo on Weathertop?

2. "But What About This Frodo?"

1. How old was Bilbo when he adopted Frodo as his heir?
2. What happened to Frodo's parents?
3. Bilbo was referred to as "well-preserved" but he tells Gandalf that he actually feels how?
4. Who would have been Bilbo's heir if he hadn't adopted Frodo?
5. When Frodo was fifty years old Gandalf came back to visit him at Bag End. How long had it been since his last visit?
6. Why did Frodo always keep the Ring on a chain?
7. If a mortal often uses the Ring to become invisible, what happens to him?
8. Who alone in history gave up the Ring willingly to someone else's care?
9. When Gandalf first told Frodo of the evils of the Ring, Frodo wanted to throw it away. What happened when he tried to do so?
10. What would happen to Frodo if Gandalf would try to force him to give up the Ring?

3. "Well, Now We're Off at Last!"

1. What day did Frodo choose for leaving the Shire?
2. Frodo needed some sort of destination for his journey. Where did Gandalf advise him to go?
3. Who did Frodo sell Bag End to?
4. Where did Frodo tell everyone in the Shire that he was going?
5. Just before Frodo left Bag End a stranger stopped to ask Ham Gamgee about Frodo. Who was the stranger?
6. In the Woody End, a Black Rider was crawling toward Frodo, Sam, and Pippin when he was startled away by singing. Who was singing?
7. Why was Frodo afraid of Farmer Maggot?
8. Buckland was originally unprotected on the east. What did the Bucklanders build there and what was its name?
9. In Old Forest, Merry and Pippin fell asleep with their backs to an old willow tree. What did the tree do to them?
10. How did Sam propose to rescue Merry and Pippin and what was the tree's reaction?

4. "There's Something Funny about All This"

1. Who had stopped at Farmer Maggot's just before Frodo got there and what did he want?
2. How did Tom Bombadil rescue Merry and Pippin from the willow tree?
3. When they prepared to leave his house, what place did Tom Bombadil tell the hobbits to avoid?
4. On the way to East Road, the hobbits were captured. By whom?
5. An arm was creeping toward Sam preparing to kill him. What did Frodo do?
6. The ponies Merry provided for their journey had no names. Who finally named them?
7. What name did Frodo go by at the inn in Bree?
8. Frodo sang a song at the inn to prevent Pippin from finishing a story about Bilbo. What happened as he sang the song a second time?
9. What was the message Gandalf left at Bree and when was it supposed to be given to Frodo?
10. Merry followed a Black Rider almost to the gate of Bree. He was found lying by the roadside. What happened to him?

5. "There Were Mysterious Wanderers"

1. The hobbits lost their ponies at the inn in Bree. Whom did they finally buy a baggage pony from and how much did it cost?
2. Who left the beryl as a token on the Last Bridge?
3. What happened to Frodo at the Ford of Rivendell when the leader of the Black Riders raised up his hand to him?
4. Frodo was across the Ford of Rivendell and the Black Riders were coming after him. What happened while they were still in the water that saved Frodo from capture?
5. Which one of the thirteen Dwarves that had been in Thorin Oakenshield's Company did Frodo meet at Rivendell and why was he there?
6. What news did Radagast the Brown bring to Gandalf the Grey?
7. How did Gandalf escape from Orthanc?
8. What happened while the Company of the Ring camped at the borders of Hollin that made them feel that the area was not wholesome after all?
9. Why did the Company turn back after only going part of the way up Caradhras?
10. What path did the Company take when they had to turn away from Caradhras?

6. "Down into the Land of Shadow"

1. What did Frodo keep hearing in Moria?
2. Who attacked the Company while they were in the Chamber of Mazarbul?
3. By what means did the Company cross the Celebrant River?
4. What did the numbers of the Company feel when the Lady Galadriel held them each in her gaze?
5. Who was following them down the river Anduin?
6. What happened when the Company headed for shore at Sarn Gebir?
7. At Rauros the Company was to decide whether to go west to Minas Tirith or east to Mordor or to split up and do both. What did Frodo decide?
8. What did Frodo feel on Amon Hen when he looked east to Barad-dûr?
9. What did Boromir want Frodo to do?
10. What did Sam see when he hurried back to Parth Galen looking for Frodo?

QUOTATIONS

1. "Servant of the Secret Fire"

Who said the following and on what occasion:

1. "I doubt very much if your friends would be in danger if you were not with them! The pursuit would follow you and leave us in peace, I think. It is you, Frodo, and that which you bear that brings us all in peril."

2. "I am a servant of the Secret Fire, wielder of the flame of Anor. You cannot pass. The dark fire will not avail you, flame of Udûn. Go back to the Shadow! You cannot pass."

3. "Alas for the folly of these days! Here all are enemies of the one Enemy, and yet I must walk blind, while the sun is merry in the woodland under leaves of gold!"

4. "How it angers me! Fool! Obstinate Fool! Running willfully to death and ruining our cause. If any mortals have claim to the Ring, it is the men of Númenor, and not Halflings. It is not yours save by unhappy chance. It might have been mine. It should be mine."

5. "There's something fishy in this, my dear! I believe that mad Baggins is off again. Silly old fool. But why worry? He hasn't taken the vittles with him."

6. "Well, what next? I have heard of strange doings in this land, but I have seldom heard of a Hobbit sleeping out of doors under a tree."

7. "The Company of the Ring shall be Nine; and the Nine Walkers shall be set against the Nine Riders that are evil. With you and your faithful servant, Gandalf will go; for this shall be his great task, and maybe the end of his labours."

8. "Just a plain Hobbit you look. But there is more about you now than appears on the surface."

9. "He is the Bearer, and the fate of the Burden is on him. I do not think that it is our part to drive him one way or the other. Nor do I think that we should succeed, if we tried. There are other powers at work far stronger."

10. "Take off your golden ring! Your hand's more fair without it. Come back! Leave your game and sit down beside me! We must talk a while more, and think about the morning."

2. "You... You're a Brandybuck!"

1. "And yet it would be a relief in a way not to be bothered with it any more. It has been so growing on my mind lately. Sometimes I have felt it was like an eye looking at me."
2. "You'll live to regret it, young fellow! Why didn't you go too? You don't belong here; you're no Baggins — you — you're a Brandybuck!"
3. "Deserves it! I daresay he does. Many that live deserve death. And some that die deserve life. Can you give it to them?"
4. "Don't let him hurt me, sir! Don't let him turn me into anything unnatural! My old dad would take on so. I meant no harm, on my honour, sir!"
5. "That Gandalf should be late does not bode well. But it is said: Do not meddle in the affairs of wizards, for they are subtle and quick to anger."
6. "We were both right! The short cut has gone crooked already; but we got under cover only just in time."
7. "There's earth under his old feet, and clay on his fingers; wisdom in his bones, and both his eyes are open."
8. "Old knives are long enough as swords for hobbit-people. Sharp blades are good to have, if Shire-folk go walking, east, south, or far away into dark and danger."
9. "Is there no escape then? If I move I shall be seen and hunted! If I stay, I shall draw them to me!"
10. "In which case it is no longer white. And he that breaks a thing to find out what it is has left the path of wisdom."

3. "Power of the Dark Lord!"

1. "It is true that if these hobbits understood the danger they would not dare to go. But they would still wish to go, or wish that they dared, and be shamed and unhappy."
2. "You should fear the many eyes of the servants of Sauron. I do not doubt that news of the discomfiture of the Riders has already reached him, and he will be filled with wrath."
3. "I too once passed the Dimrill Gate, but though I also came out again, the memory is very evil. I do not wish to enter Moria a second time."
4. "Many have received worse than this in payment for the slaying of their first orc. The cut is not poisoned, as the wounds of orc-blades too often are."
5. "Against my will we passed under the shades of Moria, to our loss. And now we must enter the Golden Wood, you say. But of that perilous land we have heard in Gondor, and it is said that few come out who once go in."
6. "Indeed in nothing is the power of the Dark Lord more clearly shown than in the estrangement that divides all those who still oppose him."
7. "Nothing, unless it might be—unless it is permitted to ask, nay, to name a single strand of your hair, which surpasses the gold of the earth as the stars surpass the gems of the mine."
8. "What it was I cannot guess, but I have never felt such a challenge. The counter-spell was terrible. It nearly broke me."
9. "Yet even so, as Ring-bearer and as one that had borne it on finger and seen that which is hidden, your sight is grown keener. You have perceived my thought more clearly than many that are accounted wise."
10. "You are forgetting not only your family history, but all you ever knew about trolls. It is broad daylight with a bright sun, and yet you come back trying to scare me with a tale of live trolls waiting for us in this glade!"

TRIVIA

1. "The World Was Fair"

1. What did Bilbo leave to Old Rory Brandybuck?
2. How many signatures did a Hobbit will require?
3. Frodo warned Sam Gamgee to tell no one what he had overheard. What did he say that Gandalf would turn Sam into if he did tell?
4. How old was Lobelia Sacksville-Baggins when she took possession of Bag End?
5. On the way to Buckland, how long did Frodo, Sam, and Pippin travel before their first rest break?
6. At what address did Samwise Gamgee and his father live?
7. What did Mrs. Maggot have Farmer Maggot give to Frodo?
8. While he was sleeping at Crickhollow, Frodo dreamed he heard a sound that he had often dreamed about before. What was it that he dreamed he heard?
9. What part of Old Forest does Merry say is the queerest part of the whole wood?
10. What did Tom Bombadil keep from the Barrow-wight's pile of treasure?

2. "The Mountains Tall"

1. What were the names given to Merry's five ponies?
2. Bob and Nob gave Sam a parting gift when he and the others set out for Rivendell from Bree. What was it?
3. What did Frodo cry out as he struck out at the Lord of the Nazgûl on Weathertop?
4. How many days and nights did Elrond tend Frodo to heal him of the Morgul-knife wound?
5. What words did Gandalf use to light the fire on Caradhras?
6. What weapons did the Balrog wield?
7. What direction did the gates of Caras Galadan face?
8. How long had it been since Aragorn was last in Lórien?
9. Who first summoned the White Council?
10. Who wove the elf-cloth for the cloaks given to the Company in Lórien?

QUESTIONS

1. "The Orcs Were Getting Ready"

1. While looking for Frodo, Boromir, Pippin, and Merry were attacked by Orcs. What was unusual about those Orcs?
2. What did Aragorn do with Boromir's body?
3. Pippin left a sign for those who followed behind. What was it?
4. Why didn't the Rohirrim see Aragorn, Legolas, or Gimli?
5. Who authorized that horses be given to them?
6. Pippin hinted to one of the Orcs that he had the Ring. Which Orc?
7. What was the name of the place Fangorn took Merry and Pippin to on the first night and what was used to light it?
8. What had Saruman been doing to the forest that made Fangorn so angry?
9. Whom did Aragorn, Legolas, and Gimli meet in Fangorn Forest?
10. Who are the Winged Messengers?

2. "The King of the Golden Hall"

1. Why wasn't Théoden glad to see Gandalf at Meduseld?
2. Théoden was bent with age and listened to the crooked counsels of Gríma Wormtongue. What did Gandalf do and what happened to Théoden because of it?
3. Théoden told Gandalf that he could have any gift he chose. What did Gandalf ask for?
4. Who did Théoden name to be his heir and whom did he leave in charge of his people at the Golden Hall?
5. The original destination of the Riders of the Mark was the Fords of Isen. Where did they go instead?
6. When the Riders of the Mark rode forth from Helm's Gate to rout the Orcs they found the land had changed. What was different?
7. At this moment who came to the aid of the Eorlingas?
8. Why were the Hillmen of Dunland amazed at being given their freedom?
9. When Gandalf and Théoden and company got to Isengard it was in ruins. Who was there before them?
10. When the Ents journeyed to Isengard they were accompanied by creatures somewhat like themselves. What were these creatures called?

3. Flotsam and Jetsam

1. The Ents briefly rerouted the waters of the Isen. What did they do with the water?
2. What did Treebeard do with Wormtongue?
3. Gandalf came to Treebeard to get help against the Orcs attacking King Théoden. What did Treebeard do?
4. What was the effect of Saruman's voice on many of those who listened to him?
5. Gandalf told Saruman that he could leave Orthanc unharmed as long as he gave two things to Gandalf. What two things?
6. What did Wormtongue throw down from the tower of Orthanc?
7. Who guarded Orthanc to make sure Saruman didn't leave there?
8. What did Pippin do the first night they stopped on the journey back to Edoras?
9. What happened to Pippin because of it?
10. What passed overhead after the incident with Pippin?

4. Past the Marshes, Beyond the Black Gate

1. Frodo and Sam used an elf-rope with one end tied to a stump to climb down a steep gully. What happened when Sam gave it a farewell tug?
2. What was Frodo's explanation for the above? What was Sam's?
3. What did Gollum do when Sam tied his rope around Gollum's ankle?
4. What did the rope do to Gollum and why?
5. What did Frodo make Gollum swear to before he released him from the rope?
6. What did Sam see in the water of the Dead Marshes?
7. What did Gollum do when Frodo fell asleep in the pit by the slag heaps?
8. When they camped in Ithilien, Sam had Gollum get something for him. What was it and what did he do with it?
9. How did the Rangers of Ithilien find Frodo and Sam?
10. What came crashing through the trees, to Sam's terror and delight?

5. "An Evil Thing in Spider-form"

1. Whom were the Rangers of Ithilien going to fight when they found Frodo and Sam?
2. What was Faramir's relationship to Boromir?
3. Frodo and Sam were taken to Faramir's refuge. What was it called and what was just in front of it?
4. Sam told Faramir that he had an air that reminded Sam of something. What?
5. What was the name of the fields that the Men of Gondor ceded to the Rohirrim for their aid?
6. While on the path to Cirith Ungol Frodo saw the Lord of the Nazgûl. What was the Lord doing?
7. Though he was compelled to put on the Ring, Frodo resisted and grasped something else instead. What?
8. In the tunnel Frodo took the phial of Galadriel and Sting and charged against an evil being. Who was it?
9. What blocked the end of the tunnel and how did they get through it?
10. Who prevented Sam from warning Frodo about the menace of the tunnel?
11. What decision did Sam have to make after he found Frodo dead?
12. What did Sam learn about Frodo from the Orcs who took his body?

QUOTATIONS
1. "There Is Evil Afoot"
Who said the following and on what occasion:

1. "There is evil afoot in Isengard, and the West is no longer safe. It is as Gandalf feared: by some means the traitor Saruman has had news of our journey."
2. "The world is all grown strange. Elf and Dwarf in company walk in our daily fields; and folk speak with the Lady of the Wood and yet live..."
3. "My dear tender little fools, everything you have, and everything you know, will be got out of you in due time: everything! You'll wish there was more that you could tell to satisfy the Questioner, indeed you will: quite soon."
4. "Curse him, root and branch! Many of those trees were my friends, creatures I had known from nut and acorn; many had voices of their own that are lost forever now. And there are wastes of stump and bramble where once there were singing groves."
5. "The Dark Lord has Nine: But we have One, mightier than they: the White Rider. He has passed through the fire and the abyss, and they shall fear him."
6. "A burden you have been, but not so now. Light as a swan's feather in my claw you are. The Sun shines through you. Indeed I do not think you need me any more: were I to let you fall, you would float upon the wind."
7. "Do you bring men? Do you bring horses, swords, spears? That I would call aid; that is our present need. But who are these that follow at your tail? Three ragged wanderers in grey, and you yourself the most beggar-like of the four!"
8. "A witless worm you have become. Therefore be silent, and keep your forked tongue behind your teeth. I have not passed through fire and death to bandy crooked words with a serving man till the lightning falls."
9. "Most of all I owe to you, my guest. Once again you have come in time. I would give you a gift ere we go, at your own choosing. You have only to name aught that is mine. I reserve now only my sword."

10. "That is not the road that you must take. I have spoken words of hope. But only of hope. Hope is not victory. War is upon us and all our friends, a war in which only the use of the Ring could give us surety of victory."

2. "An Old Liar with Honey on His Forked Tongue?"

1. "Help now to repair the evil in which you have joined, and afterwards you shall take an oath never again to pass the Fords of Isen in arms, nor to march with the enemies of Men; and then you shall go free back to your land."
2. "And now that the great ones have gone to discuss high matters, the hunters can perhaps learn the answers to their own small riddles."
3. "Fate has not been kinder to him than he deserves. The sight of the ruin of all that he thought so strong and magnificent must have been almost punishment enough. But I fear that worse awaits him."
4. "Have we ridden forth to victory, only to stand at last amazed by an old liar with honey on his forked tongue? So would the trapped wolf speak to the hounds, if he could."
5. "Yes, when you also have the Keys of Barad-dûr itself, I suppose; and the crowns of seven kings, and the rods of the Five Wizards, and have purchased yourself a pair of boots many sizes larger than those you wear now."
6. "He has grown or something. He can be both kinder and more alarming, merrier and more solemn than before, I think. He has changed; but we have not had a chance to see how much, yet."
7. "But I don't like leaving it, and that's a fact. It goes hard parting with anything I brought out of the elf-country. Made by Galadriel herself, too, maybe."
8. "This is Sting. You have seen it before once upon a time. Let go, or you'll feel it this time! I'll cut your throat."
9. "I could trust them to shut their eyes of their own accord, but eyes will blink if the feet stumble. Lead them so they do not falter."
10. "We boast seldom, and then perform, or die in the attempt. 'Not if I found it on the highway would I take it' I said."

TRIVIA

1. "The Window on the West"

1. How far had Aragorn, Legolas, and Gimli travelled—on foot—before they met up with Éomer?
2. What was the name of the horse lent by the Rohirrim to Aragorn and who was its former owner?
3. What kind of tree made the gate to Wellinghall?
4. What were the names of the three oldest living Ents?
5. What was the name given to Gandalf by Gríma Wormtongue?
6. How tall was the Deeping Wall?
7. How many days had passed between when Pippin and Merry were captured by Orcs and when they again met up with Aragorn, Legolas, and Gimli?
8. What was the year marked on the barrels of Longbottom Leaf Pippin found at Isengard?
9. How long did Treebeard say that the Ents would guard Saruman?
10. On the fourth evening after they left the Company, Sam and Frodo came to a deep cleft. How deep was it?

2. Perils of the Journey

1. On the fifth day after they were joined by Gollum, Frodo and Sam waited for daylight to pass in a wide pit. What was at the bottom of the pit?
2. What was Sam's name for the Men from out of the South that rode oliphaunts?
3. Who was the last king to rule Gondor?
4. Name the two men Faramir left to guard Frodo and Sam.
5. What color were the scarves that Frodo's and Sam's eyes were blindfolded with?
6. What were the staves that Faramir gave to Frodo and Sam made of?
7. There were two sets of stairs leading to Cirith Ungol. What were they called?
8. What was the name of Shelob's lair?
9. What was the name of the Orc the other Orcs had found trussed up, but alive, in Shelob's lair?
10. Where was the first blow Sam struck against Shelob with Sting?

QUESTIONS

1. "Seven Stars, Seven Stones, One White Tree"

1. On how many levels was Minas Tirith built?
2. What did Pippin offer to Denethor in payment for Boromir's saving his life?
3. Before Gandalf went to the lords' council he asked Pippin to do him a favor. What?
4. Many of the Men of Gondor called Pippin Ernil i Pheriannath. What did that mean?
5. Who came riding up behind the Riders of Rohan?
6. What message did Elrond send for Aragorn?
7. How did Aragorn learn of Gondor's peril from the South?
8. What was the oath that the Men of the Mountains broke at the time of the beginning of Gondor?
9. What was the curse that followed the oath-breaking?
10. What did Aragorn do at the Stone of Erech?

2. "Ride Now, Ride Now! Ride to Gondor!"

1. What symbol did Denethor send to Théoden of Rohan to indicate Gondor's need of aid?
2. What event made Théoden decide that there was no need to hide his army's journey to Gondor?
3. What one request did Aragorn make to Éowyn before he left for the Paths of the Dead?
4. When Théoden refused to allow Merry to accompany him to Minas Tirith, who offered to hide him and take him along?
5. When Faramir returned to Minas Tirith, he was pursued. Who tried to stop him and who rescued him?
6. Denethor was angry at Faramir because he had not brought back something. What?
7. The Orcs set up great catapults outside Minas Tirith. What missiles did these throw?
8. Why did Gandalf take command of the defenses of Minas Tirith?
9. Who walked about the City helping to chase away the dread for a brief while?
10. Although Faramir was not yet dead, what did Denethor decide to do?

3. "Lord of the Black Land Come Forth!"

1. What was the weakest point in the wall around Minas Tirith?
2. While camped a day's ride from Minas Tirith, Merry heard drums. Whose drums were they?
3. What aid did Ghân-buri-Ghân offer to Théoden?
4. What did the Wild Man want as a reward?
5. What did Théoden's scouts find that made him believe that Denethor knew nothing of the Rohirrim's journey?
6. What did the wind that blew up from the Sea do?
7. Who was the only one standing when the Lord of the Nazgûl came for Théoden?
8. What happened to all the others who were to guard Théoden?
9. How was it that the Lord of the Nazgûl, who could not fall by the hand of man, was killed?
10. What was the means of Théoden's death?

4. "War Now Calls Us!"

1. Who came from the South in ships with black sails?
2. Who stood alone at the door to Denethor's tomb to prevent it being set on fire?
3. Although Sauron could not subdue the will of Denethor he did cause him to feel great despair and go mad. How?
4. What injury did Merry sustain?
5. What did Aragorn do after the battle was over and what did this action prove to the people of Gondor?
6. When the Dead did battle with the Haradrim at the Great River they had no need for swords or lances. What weapon did they have that none could withstand?
7. What happened to speed the ships up the River to Minas Tirith?
8. Why did Aragorn use the Stone of Orthanc to show himself to Sauron?
9. What does Gandalf say that Sauron will think if they should march out and attack him?
10. When some of his men were so badly affected by horror that they could not walk, what did Aragorn tell them?

5. "Towers Strong and High"

1. When the army reached the Black Gate they called Sauron forth to surrender. Who came out of the Gate to answer?
2. What happened when Aragorn held the eyes of this messenger?
3. What tokens did the messenger have to show them?
4. When the messenger fled back to the Gate he gave a signal. What then happened?
5. How did Pippin become injured?
6. What was happening just as Pippin lost consciousness?
7. When Sam saw the Tower of Cirith Ungol he suddenly realized that its purpose wasn't to keep enemies out of Mordor. What was its purpose?
8. How did Sam get past the Two Watchers of the Tower of Cirith Ungol?
9. What did they do after he got past them?
10. Although a whole garrison of Orcs was stationed at the Tower of Cirith Ungol Sam got to Frodo almost without a fight. Why?

6. "The Crack of Doom"

1. What happened to the gateway that the Watchers guarded when Sam and Frodo escaped from the Tower of Cirith Ungol?
2. Who was the first to answer the Watchers' Alarm?
3. What did Sam say he would ask of Galadriel if she could hear him?
4. Was his request answered?
5. What happened after Sam and Frodo had been walking along a road for a while?
6. How did Sam and Frodo escape from the above situation?
7. Finally at the foot of Orodruin Frodo's strength gave out and he could walk no farther. What did Sam do?
8. As Frodo and Sam started along the path to the Crack of Doom they were attacked. Who attacked them?
9. What did Frodo do when he reached the Crack of Doom?
10. What effect did Frodo's action have on Sauron?

7. "The Ring-bearer Has Fulfilled His Quest"

1. How did the Ring end up in the Fire?
2. How did Sam and Frodo escape from Orodruin before they were engulfed in molten rock?
3. On what day will the New Year in Gondor begin now?
4. What clothes did Gandalf tell Frodo and Sam to wear to meet the King?
5. Who found Pippin on the battlefield and how did he happen to be found?
6. Three people were involved in the crowning of Aragorn. Who presented the crown to him? Who brought it to him? And who set it upon his head?
7. What penalty did the King give to Beregond for spilling blood in the Hollows?
8. What day was Aragorn waiting for?
9. On the slope of Mount Mindolluin Aragorn found a sign of hope for the realm of Gondor. What was it?
10. What did Arwen tell Frodo that he could do in her stead?

8. Partings

1. What gift did Éowyn give to Merry to remember Dernhelm by as he prepared to leave Edoras?
2. Where did the ending of the Fellowship of the Ring occur?
3. Where were Legolas and Gimli going and why?
4. Whom did the remaining members of the Company encounter on the sixth day after leaving Aragorn?
5. The hobbits and Gandalf reached Rivendell in time for what celebration?
6. Why did the hobbits have to keep repeating their stories to Bilbo?
7. What parting gifts did Bilbo give to Frodo, Sam, Merry, and Pippin as they prepared to leave Rivendell?
8. Gandalf wasn't going to the Shire with the hobbits. Where was he going instead?
9. When the hobbits got to the Brandywine Bridge they found a locked gate. Who opened the gate?
10. What did Merry order the gate-opener to do then?

9. Trouble at the Shire

1. When the hobbits got to the edge of the village of Frogmorton they found their way was blocked. By whom and why?
2. What was the four hobbits' reaction to this?
3. Why did the ruffians in Bywater give way before Merry, Pippin, and Sam?
4. How did Merry call the Shire to arms?
5. Before he was ready to fight Sam had to talk to someone. Who?
6. Who first brought the ruffians to the Shire? Why?
7. Who did Sharkey turn out to be?
8. Why did he try to destroy the Shire?
9. What did he foretell for Frodo?
10. When Lobelia Sackville-Baggins died she left all her money to Frodo. What was he to use it for?

10. "The End of Fellowship in the Middle-earth"

1. What was the only thing Frodo did as Deputy Mayor?
2. What did Sam do with Galadriel's gift?
3. What was the result?
4. What happened to Frodo every October the sixth? Every March thirteenth?
5. What name did Frodo suggest for Sam's first child?
6. On Bilbo's birthday, where were Elrond, Galadriel, Bilbo, and Frodo going?
7. Who met them there?
8. What Elven treasures went with them?
9. Who came to ride back with Sam?
10. What did Frodo give to Sam before they parted?

QUOTATIONS

1. "We Must Ride Our Own Road"

Who said the following and on what occasion:

1. "But though all the signs forebode that the doom of Gondor is drawing nigh, less now to me is that darkness than my own darkness."
2. "He's bold, more bold than many deem; for in these days men are slow to believe that a captain can be wise and learned in the scrolls of lore and song, as he is, and yet a man of hardihood and swift judgement in the field."
3. "I am no warrior at all and dislike any thought of battle; but waiting on the edge of one that I can't escape is worst of all."
4. "We must ride our own road and no longer in secret. For me the time of stealth has passed. I will ride east by the swiftest way, and I will take the Paths of the Dead."
5. "It is a long way to run; but run I shall, if I cannot ride, even if I wear my feet off and arrive weeks too late."
6. "For Boromir was loyal to me and no wizard's pupil. He would have remembered his father's need, and would not have squandered what fortune gave."
7. "No tomb! No long slow sleep of death embalmed. We will burn like heathen kings before ever a ship sailed hither from the West."
8. "Old fool! This is my hour. Do you not know Death when you see it? Die now and curse in vain!"
9. "Well, you must choose between orders and the life of Faramir. And as for others, I think you have a madman to deal with, not a lord."
10. "I am not a tree-root, Sir, nor a bag, but a bruised hobbit. The least you can do in amends is to tell me what is afoot."

2. "The Houses of Lamentation"

1. "He will bear thee away to the houses of lamentation, beyond all darkness, where thy flesh shall be devoured, and thy shrivelled mind be left naked to the Lidless Eye."
2. "You stand between me and my lord and kin. Begone, if you be not deathless! For living or dark undead, I will smite you, if you touch him."
3. "So you spoke, but hope oft deceives, and I knew not then that you were a man foresighted. Yet twice blessed is help unlooked for, and never was a meeting of friends more joyful."
4. "Thou hadst already stolen half my son's love. Now thou stealest the hearts of my knights also, so that they rob me wholly of my son at the last."
5. "But it is the way of my people to use light words at such times and say less than they mean. We fear to say too much. It robs us of the right words when a jest is out of place."
6. "The weed is better than I thought. It reminds me of the roses of Imloth Melui when I was a lass, and no king could ask for better."
7. "It is ever so with the things that Men begin: there is a frost in Spring, or a blight in Summer, and they fail of their promise."
8. "But deep in the hearts of all my kindred lies the sea-longing, which it is perilous to stir. Alas! For the gulls. No peace shall I have again under beech or under elm."
9. "But we must at all costs keep his Eye from his true peril. We cannot achieve victory by arms, but by arms we can give the Ringbearer his only chance, frail though it be."
10. "Surely, this is the greatest jest in all the history of Gondor: that we should ride with seven thousands, scarcely as many as the vanguard of its army in the days of its power, to assail the mountains and the impenetrable gate of the Black Land."

3. "A Piece of Elvish Glass"

1. "It needs more to make a king than a piece of elvish glass, or a rabble such as this. Why? Any brigand of the hills can show as good a following!"
2. "You have naught to fear from us, until your errand is done. But unless your master has come to new wisdom, then with all his servants you will be in great peril."
3. "You are the fool, going on hoping and toiling. You could have lain down and gone to sleep together days ago, if you hadn't been so dogged. But you'll die just the same, or worse."
4. "Thrice shall pay for all, if you are willing. You will not find me a burden much greater than when you bore me from Zirak-zigil . . ."
5. "How do I feel? Well, I don't know how to say it. I feel, I feel, I feel like spring after winter, and sun on the leaves; and like trumpets and harps and all the songs I have ever heard!"
6. "Minas Ithil in Morgul-vale shall be utterly destroyed, and though it may in time to come be made clean, no man may dwell there for many long years."
7. "Many folk like to know before-hand what is to be set on the table; but those who have laboured to prepare the feast like to keep their secret; for wonder makes the words of praise louder."
8. "The Third Age was my age. I was the Enemy of Sauron; and my work is finished. I shall go soon."
9. "Nay, you are excused for my part, lord. You have chosen the Evening; but my love is given to the Morning. And my heart forbodes that soon it will pass away forever."
10. "Since the day when you rose before me out of the green grass of the downs I have loved you, and that love shall not fail. But now I must depart for a while to my own realm, where there is much to heal and set in order."

4. "Go in Peace!"

1. "You may be right, but this snake had still one tooth left, I think. He had the poison of his voice, and I guess that he persuaded you..."
2. "It is sad that we should meet only thus at the ending. For the world is changing: I feel it in the water, I feel it in the earth, and I smell it in the air. I do not think we shall meet again."
3. "This is only a repayment in token; for you took more, I'll be bound. Still, a beggar must be grateful, if a thief returns him even a morsel of his own."
4. "I fear it may be so with mine. There is no real going back. Though I may come to the Shire, it will not seem the same; for I shall not be the same."
5. "And as for you, my dear friends, you will need no help. You are grown up now. Grown indeed very high; among the great you are, and I have no longer any fear at all for any of you."
6. "We have left all the rest behind, one after another. It seems almost like a dream that has slowly faded."
7. "Don't be absurd! I am going where I please, and in my own time. I happen to be going to Bag End on business, but if you insist on going too, well that is your affair."
8. "He was great once, of a noble kind that we should not dare to raise our hands against. He is fallen, and his cure is beyond us; but I would still spare him, in the hope that he may find it."
9. "I tried to save the Shire, and it has been saved, but not for me."
10. "Well, here at last, dear friends, on the shores of the Sea comes the end of our fellowship in Middle-earth. Go in peace!"

TRIVIA

1. The Sounds of War

1. What was the name of the wall that surrounded the fields of the Pelennor and Minas Tirith?
2. How long does Pippin tell Beregond it will be before he "comes of age?"
3. Which company did Beregond belong to?
4. What color was the standard that Aragorn bade Halbarad unfurl at the Stone of Erech?
5. Name the errand-rider of Denethor that delivered the token of war to Théoden.
6. What was the name of the door to the Tombs of Gondor?
7. What was the name of the great battering ram used at Minas Tirith?
8. What was the battering ram named after?
9. Who alone among the free horses could withstand the terror of the Nazgûl?
10. What did seeing Ghân-buri-Ghân remind Merry of?

2. Who and What

1. What was the name of Théoden's banner-bearer?
2. What was the standard of the Haradrim?
3. When Aragorn used the athelas to heal Faramir, Éowyn, and Merry, it had a different scent each time it was put in boiling water. Describe the three scents.
4. How many great ships of Umbar were at Pelargir when Aragorn attacked?
5. Who led the scouts for the Captains of the West on the journey to Morannon?
6. What was the name of the Orc that Sam frightened on the stairs of Minas Morgul?
7. Who was the only Orc to survive after the battle between the two companies of Orcs at the tower of Cirith Ungol?
8. What was the password Sam and Frodo used when Sam went to look for supplies in the tower?
9. On what day did Sam and Frodo awaken after they were rescued from Mount Doom?
10. What did Arwen Evenstar give to Frodo to help soothe the memories of darkness?

A–I. Kingdoms of the Middle-earth

1. Name the two kingdoms founded in Middle-earth by the Faithful of Númenor.
2. Who was the High King of the Faithful who ruled both kingdoms with his sons?
3. What gifts from the Elves did the Faithful bring to Middle-earth?
4. The North-kingdom was divided into three realms after Eärendur. Which was the only one where the line of Isildur continued?
5. Who gave food and shelter to King Arvedui when he fled north from the power of Angmar?
6. Who was the lord of Angmar?
7. What happened to the ship that rescued Arvedui?
8. The North-kingdom ended because the Dúnedain were diminished but the line of the kings was continued. How?
9. What were the four heirlooms of the Kings that were kept at Rivendell?
10. What was the cause of the Kin-strife in the southern kingdom?

A–II. Notes from a Loremaster's Journal

1. Who overthrew Eldacar during the Kin-strife?
2. Where did the enemies of the king set up a refuge after the Kin-strife?
3. What happened during the reign of Telemnar that killed him, his children, and many of his people?
4. What group of peoples invaded the southern kingdom and waged a war of nearly one hundred years?
5. Who was given the crown of the southern kingdom when the king and his sons were slain in the war?
6. Who had claimed the crown but was refused?
7. How did the Witch-king shame Eärnur?
8. What became of Eärnur, the last king?
9. Who ruled in his stead?
10. Since rule of the southern kingdom had passed from the kings, who now ruled Gondor?

A–III. Who, What, and When

1. What Steward gave Saruman the keys to Isengard?
2. When Belecthor II died what also died and could not be replaced?
3. On what one matter of advice to Ecthelion did Thorongil and Denethor II disagree?
4. Who were Aragorn's parents?
5. Why did the meara Mansbane—renamed Felaróf—allow Eorl to ride him?
6. What did Helm Hammerhand and Freca argue about that ended in Freca's death?
7. Who led an invasion against Rohan four years later and set himself up as king?
8. Why did Helm go amongst his enemies unarmed?
9. Who were Théoden's parents and where did his mother come from?
10. What gift did Elessar renew to Éomer that ceded Elessar's kingship over Rohan and what did Éomer in turn renew?

B. Legends of the Ages

1. What event ended the First Age?
2. What event ended the Second Age?
3. When did the Third Age end and the Fourth Age begin?
4. In 1436 King Elessar came north to the Brandywine Bridge. What gift did he give to Sam?
5. After Rose died Sam left the Shire. Where is it said that he went?
6. What did Sam give to Elanor before he left?
7. Who sent for Meriadoc when he was 102 years old?
8. Who went with Meriadoc, never again to be seen in the Shire?
9. When King Elessar died, whose bodies were laid to rest beside his?
10. After King Elessar died Legolas sailed over the Sea. Who reportedly went with him?

QUESTIONS

1. "The Beginning of Days"

1. Which of the Valar did Melkor hate and fear most?
2. Who created the Two Trees of Valinor?
3. Who were the Children of Ilúvatar? Who were the Firstborn?
4. Who kept destroying all the works of the Valar on Middle-earth? Why?
5. Why were the Dwarves made?
6. What one of her creations did Yavanna hold dearest? And what was created to protect them?
7. What did the Valar do with Melkor after his capture?
8. What were the Elves who went with Oromë called?
9. What did Ulmo do that turned the Elves' fear of the Sea into desire?
10. Why did Melkor hate the Elves?

2. "The Darkening"

1. Why did the Valar release Melkor from bondage?
2. What happened to any mortal flesh or anything of evil that touched the Silmarils?
3. What was Fëanor's punishment for drawing his sword against a kinsman?
4. Did Fëanor agree to give the Silmarils to Yavanna?
5. What servants of Melkor saved him from Ungoliant?
6. What did Morgoth do with the Silmarils?
7. What oath did Fëanor and his seven sons make, calling the Everlasting Dark upon themselves if they did not keep it?
8. What was the cause of the Kinslaying at Alqualondë?
9. Which of Finwë's three sons returned to Valinor after Mandos proclaimed the Doom of the Noldor?
10. What event was the first fulfillment of the Prophecy?

3. Lore of the Ancients

1. What was the name of the dwelling that the Dwarves delved for Thingol?
2. Against whom did the Sindar fight in the first battle of the Wars of Beleriand?
3. What was the Girdle of Melian?
4. What did Varda create the Sun and the Moon from?
5. What two peoples fought in the second battle of the Wars of Beleriand?
6. Maedhros was fastened upon Thangorodrim by a band of steel around his wrist. Who set him free and how?
7. Before Turgon left for Gondolin, Ulmo advised him to leave something behind in Nevrast. What and why?
8. Who was the first of the Noldor to discover Men?
9. What was Amlach's quarrel with Morgoth?
10. What did Finrod Felagund give to Barahir as a token of aid and friendship?

4. "The Hidden King"

1. Who went to Angband and challenged Morgoth?
2. Who prevented Morgoth from throwing that person's body to the wolves?
3. How did Húrin and Huor come to Gondolin?
4. How did Sauron capture Gorlim?
5. What did Gorlim reveal to Sauron?
6. Why did Beren eat no flesh?
7. What did Thingol order Beren to bring him before he could wed Lúthien?
8. Whose aid did Beren enlist in his task?
9. Who did Lúthien ask for help in saving Beren and what did he do to her?
10. How often could Huan the hound speak with words before his death?

5. "Tales of Sorrow"

1. Who helped Lúthien escape from Nargothrond?
2. When the werewolf of Sauron came to eat Beren what happened?
3. In what form did Sauron battle Huan? Who triumphed?
4. Who was Huan's master in Middle-earth and when did Huan forsake his service?
5. What happened when Beren clapped the Silmaril in his hand?
6. What happened to Beren when he held the Silmaril before Carcharoth?
7. What did the Silmaril do to Carcharoth?
8. In the battle of Carcharoth and Huan, Huan slew Carcharoth but his own doom was fulfilled. What was the doom of Huan?
9. Before Beren died what did Lúthien ask of him?
10. Which of the choices Manwë offered to her did Lúthien take?

6. "The Doom Lies in Yourself"

1. What was the treachery of Ulfang?
2. Why did Húrin and Huor want Turgon to flee the battle?
3. Where did Morwen, wife of Húrin, send her son, Túrin, to be raised?
4. Where was the dwelling of Mîm, where Túrin later stayed?
5. Why did Túrin slay Beleg?
6. What happened to Túrin when he looked Glaurung in the eye?
7. Who was Níniel, wife of Túrin Turambar?
8. What did Níniel do when she found out who she was?
9. How did Túrin die?
10. What did the blade Gurthang say it had to avenge against Túrin?

7. Elves and Men

1. Who took Morgoth's veil from Húrin's eyes?
2. What did Húrin give Thingol as a memorial of himself?
3. How did Húrin get the token he gave Thingol?
4. What change did Thingol want made to Húrin's gift?
5. What happened when the change was completed?
6. What did Tuor find at Vinyamar?
7. Why did Voronwë lead Tuor to Gondolin?
8. What advice did Túrin bring to Turgon from Ulmo?
9. The union of Beren and Lúthien was the first union of Elf and Man. Whose was the second?
10. Who betrayed Gondolin to Morgoth?

8. The War of Wrath

1. What did Morgoth promise to give Maeglin?
2. How did some of the people of Gondolin escape?
3. Why did Eärendil want to find Valinor?
4. What did Manwë decree for Eärendil, Elwing, and their sons?
5. Eärendil was not allowed to return to Middle-earth. What was the task given to him by Manwë?
6. What did the Valar do in answer to Eärendil's plea?
7. What happened when Ancalagon fell to Middle-earth, slain?
8. Where did the Valar exile Melkor to?
9. What happened to the face of the World after the Great Battle?
10. What happened to the three Silmarils?

TRIVIA

1. Elves, Dwarves, and Balrogs

1. Which of the Eldar created the first written characters?
2. What was the name of the pearl as big as a dove's egg that Thingol gave to the Dwarves of Belegost?
3. What was the name of Eärendil's ship?
4. How many times did Fingolfin wound Morgoth?
5. What was the Sindarin name for Sauron?
6. What was another name for the Balrogs?
7. How many men would go with Finrod Felagund to aid Beren?
8. What were the names of the two lamps that Aulë built to light Middle-earth?
9. What was the name of the second battle of the Wars of Beleriand?
10. What was Cabed-en-Aras called after Nienor leaped to her death there?

AKALLABÊTH

1. What was given to the Edain for their loyalty in the fight against Morgoth?
2. Who was the first King of the Dúnedain?
3. What was the Ban of the Valar?
4. How did the King's Men and the Faithful differ?
5. Whom did Sauron convince Ar-Pharazôn to worship instead of Eru?
6. What did Isildur do when he learned that the King was going to cut down the White Tree?
7. What preparations did Elendil make at Amandil's bidding?
8. What happened to Aman after Ar-Pharazôn claimed it as his own?
9. What did Ilúvatar do to Númenor?
10. Who escaped the havoc, by the grace of the Valar?

PEOPLE – FAIR FRIENDS AND FIERCE FOES

1. Aragorn

1. By what name was Aragorn known to Frodo?
2. What was he called in Rivendell and by Bilbo, and what was its meaning?
3. How old was Aragorn when he died?
4. Where was Aragorn raised?
5. What name was he given to hide his lineage from Sauron?
6. Elrond would not allow Arwen to marry Aragorn unless he became what?
7. What was the name of Aragorn's only son and heir?
8. What was the kingdom ruled by Aragorn called?
9. Under what name did Aragorn serve in Gondor under the Steward Ecthelion II, father of Denethor?
10. Aragorn chose the Quenya version of the name in question 1 to be the name of his house. What was the name of his house to be?

2. Bilbo Baggins

1. How did Bilbo find the Ring?
2. What made Bilbo decide to go on this adventure?
3. Bilbo felt much fiercer and bolder after doing something all by himself. What?
4. How did Bilbo escape from the Wood-elves?
5. What did Bilbo do early in the Battle of the Five Armies?
6. Just as the Eagles came to the aid of the Company in the Battle of the Five Armies, what was it that happened to Bilbo?
7. Bilbo didn't want any of the treasure of Thorin but finally agreed to take something. What did he take?
8. When Bilbo arrived back at Bag End what was happening?
9. Bilbo left Bag End on his eleventy-first birthday. Where did he go?
10. While living at Bag End, what did he use the magic ring for?

3. Bilbo's Birthday

1. What month and day was Bilbo's birthday?
2. How old was Frodo on Bilbo's eleventy-first birthday?
3. What day of the week was Bilbo's eleventy-first birthday?
4. At Bilbo's birthday there were hundreds of musical crackers that bore the mark of where they were made. Where were these crackers made?
5. How many hobbits were invited to the special family dinner-party?
6. Why was that specific number chosen?
7. There was a special firework used as the signal for supper. What was it like?
8. The magnificent invitations were written in what color ink?
9. Who was in charge of the fireworks?
10. What was Bilbo's ANNOUNCEMENT?

4. Tom Bombadil

1. Who was Tom's lady?
2. When Frodo asked her, who did she say Tom was?
3. What brought Tom down to the Withywindle where Frodo found him?
4. Why was it raining the first morning the hobbits spent at Tom Bombadil's?
5. Tom walked through the rain waving his arms about. Why?
6. Who did Tom say he was?
7. How long had Tom been on Middle-earth?
8. Tom knew a lot about the Shire. Who did he owe his recent knowledge to?
9. What happened when Tom put the Ring on his finger?
10. Elves, Dwarves, and Northern Men each had their own names for Tom Bombadil. What were these names?

5. Fair Friends of Fierce Foes

1. An old man with bushy eyebrows, a pointed blue hat, long grey cloak, silver scarf, and long white beard.
2. A huge man with a thick black beard and hair, great bare arms and legs of knotted muscle, wearing a wool tunic to his knees.
3. Man-like, with bright blue eyes and a long brown beard, a red face creased with laugh lines, great yellow boots, and a blue coat.
4. A tall man, dark haired and grey-eyed, with a stern face, wearing a collar of silver set with a single white stone and bearing a great horn tipped with silver.
5. Fourteen feet high with a tall head and almost no neck, large seven-toed feet, and a sweeping, bushy grey beard. Solemn eyes and a deep, deep voice.
6. A tall man bent with age, with long, braided white hair beneath a circlet of gold set with a single diamond, a snowy beard, and sharp eyes.
7. A squat, gnarled man with a scraggly beard, short-legged, fat-armed, clad in grass around his waist.

6. Dwarves

1. Unlike Elves and Men, the Dwarves weren't created solely by Eru. Who else had a hand in their creation?
2. What was the name of the Dwarves' greatest city?
3. The discovery of what substance made the Dwarves fabulously rich?
4. Who were the Dwarves' most deadly enemies?
5. What type of weapon did they generally use?
6. Who was the eldest and most royal of the Seven Fathers?
7. Who gave the key of Erebor to Gandalf? (It was later given to Thorin and Company for their expedition.)
8. One Dwarf boldly asked Galadriel for a strand of her hair, and got it. Who was he?
9. The Dwarvish language was a secret language used only among themselves. What was it called?
10. What was the Elven name for the Dwarves?

7. More Dwarves

1. Why were those heirs of Durin that looked like him also named Durin?
2. Dwarves didn't bury their dead in earth. What did they bury them in?
3. So many died in the Battle of Azanulbizar that the dead had to be taken care of another way. How?
4. Who was the only dwarf-woman named?
5. Why weren't dwarf-women noticed when they went on a journey?
6. What number of the dwarf-men take wives?
7. What did Gimli become lord of, after the fall of Sauron?
8. What did Gimli's people make the new gates to Minas Tirith of?
9. During the War of the Ring, which Dwarf led the defense of Erebor and Dale?
10. Which Dwarf visited Bilbo after the expedition to Erebor?

8. Elves

1. Elves didn't sleep. What did they do instead?
2. Elves loved all beautiful things but especially what?
3. When the Elves grew tired of the perils of Middle-earth where did they go?
4. Who was the builder of the ships that sailed from Grey Havens in the First Age?
5. Name the Noldorin Elf who created the Silmarils.
6. What were each of the three Kindred of the Eldar called?
7. Who was the mightiest and the noblest Elf in Middle-earth in the Third Age?
8. Name the first three keepers of the Three Rings.
9. Who was the greatest King of the Grey-elves during the First Age?
10. Name the Sindarin princess who aided Beren in recovering one of the Silmarils.

9. More Elves

1. Why do Elves seldom give advice, according to Gildor Inglorion?
2. Who was the only Elf of the First Age to die a mortal death?
3. Who is accounted the wisest of the Elves of Middle-earth, the giver of gifts beyond the power of kings?
4. What creature was made as a mockery of Elves?
5. Which of the Peredhil, the half-elven, chose to belong to the Elven race?
6. Who were the first three Elves ever to go to Valinor?
7. Match each of these divisions of Elves with the meaning of its name.
   A. Vanyar   1. Elves of Darkness
   B. Noldor   2. Elves of Twilight
   C. Moriquendi   3. Fair Elves
   D. Sindar   4. Green-elves
   E. Laiquendi   5. Deep Elves
8. Why did Fëanor have neither burial nor tomb?
9. What were those Elves who never went to the Blessed Realm called?
10. What was the name of the group of Elves that were beloved by Manwë and Varda?

10. Ents

1. What are Ents?
2. Why are there so few Ents left?
3. What is Entmoot and where is it?
4. Which creature did the Enemy create as a mockery to Ents?
5. How did Ents sleep and what did they eat?
6. Arrows and poison could not harm Ents but they could be wounded seriously. By what?
7. How do Ents destroy rock?
8. Which Ent caught fire at Isengard and burned like a torch?
9. What did Treebeard call Isengard after it had been landscaped?
10. Treebeard wanted Merry and Pippin to send him news if they heard something. What?

11. Gandalf the Grey

1. When Gandalf came to Middle-earth, he was given one of the Three Rings. Who gave it to him and which of the three did he have?
2. Gandalf was not his original name. What was it?
3. In Khazad-dûm Gandalf was killed. When he came back to Middle-earth he was changed. In what way?
4. How did Gandalf defend the Company of the Ring from the Wargs near Caradhras?
5. What did Saruman want Gandalf to tell him?
6. What did Saruman do when Gandalf refused?
7. What did Gandalf do to Barliman Butterbur's beer and why?
8. The second time Gandalf went to Dol Guldur to discover who the Necromancer was, he found someone else and was given something. Who and what?
9. Why did Gandalf encourage the expedition to Erebor?
10. Of what race was Gandalf and from whom did he learn patience and pity?

12. Gollum

1. Who finally captured Gollum for Gandalf?
2. While Gollum still lived with his family what did he use the Ring for?
3. What was his original name and how did he come to be called Gollum?
4. How did Gollum tell Gandalf he got the Ring?
5. Gollum left his cave to follow Bilbo. Where did Gandalf believe Gollum ended up before Aragorn captured him?
6. After Gandalf talked to him, what did he do with Gollum?
7. At the Council of Elrond, what news did Legolas tell of Gollum?
8. How did Gollum get down the face of a precipice in the Emyn Muil? (Just before Sam caught him.)
9. What did Sam call Gollum? Why?
10. Gollum led Frodo and Sam to the passage of Cirith Ungol. What was there that he didn't warn them of and why didn't he warn them?

13. Hobbits

1. Why don't hobbits wear shoes?

Match each of the three branches of hobbits with their preferred region and the type of people they associated with most.

2. Fallohides	a. flatlands	d. Dwarves
3. Harfoots	b. forests	e. Elves
4. Stoors	c. highlands	f. Men

5. Which branch of hobbits grew beards?
6. Name the two bright colors hobbits prefer most.
7. Who was the longest-lived hobbit and how long did he live?
8. Name the two tallest hobbits. Why were they so tall?
9. Who was the Stoor that found the One Ring on a riverbank at Gladden Fields?
10. Gollum was a Stoor Hobbit. What was his original name?

14. More Hobbits

1. What is a mathom?
2. Hobbits preferred windows and doors of what shape?
3. The Took family was accorded a special respect. Why?
4. How often was the Mayor of Michel Delving elected?
5. What other offices were assigned to the mayoralty?
6. At what age do hobbits "come of age"?
7. One family of hobbits was extremely offensive and greedy. Which family?
8. Who was the only one among the Wise that studied hobbit-lore?
9. Which of the three branches of hobbits did the two founders of the Shire come from?
10. What was Man's name for hobbits?
11. In what way were the Bucklanders different from the other hobbits of the Shire?

15. Famous Hobbits

1. Who was it that charged the ranks of Goblins of Mount Gram in the Battle of Greenfields?
2. Who grew the first true pipe-weed in the Shire?
3. Who was known as the Gaffer and what was his job?
4. Who were Frodo's parents?
5. Name the two founders of the Shire.
6. Who was it that built Brandy Hall and changed his name to Brandybuck?
7. Who was the first Shire-thain?
8. Which hobbit was made a maid of honor to Queen Arwen?
9. Who became the first Warden of Westmarch? At whose request?
10. Who was the first hobbit to be imprisoned by the Chief's Men?

16. Names

Match the name with the type of people or animal it represents.

1. Carc
2. Azog
3. Tulkas
4. Meneldor
5. Thranduil
6. Déagol
7. William Huggins
8. Radagast
9. Borin
10. Scatha

a. Hobbit
b. Dragon
c. Elf
d. Raven of Erebor
e. Vala
f. Orc
g. Dwarf
h. Eagle of the Misty Mountain
i. Istari
j. Troll

17. More Names

Match each person with the other name or names he was known by.

1. Aragorn
2. Gollum
3. Tom Bombadil
4. Fangorn
5. Sauron
6. Gandalf
7. Saruman
8. Éowyn
9. Bregalad
10. Gimli
11. Gríma

a. Thorongil
b. Treebeard
c. Curunír
d. Sméagol
e. Elessar
f. Olórin
g. Iarwain Ben-adar
h. Strider
i. Lock-bearer
j. Black Hand
k. Trahald
l. Orald
m. Wormtongue
n. Quickbeam
o. Necromancer
p. Dernhelm
q. Mithrandir

18. The Nazgûl

1. How many Nazgûl were there?
2. How did they become servants of Sauron?
3. How long were the Nazgûl enslaved?
4. What was the name of the kingdom of the Lord of the Nazgûl?
5. Name the battle of the War of the Rings in which the Lord of the Nazgûl was destroyed.
6. Sauron sent the Nazgûl to the Shire in Third Age 3018 for what reason?
7. Where did Frodo and the Lord of the Nazgûl do battle?
8. What were the only weapons that could wound the Nazgûl?
9. When was their power strongest?
10. How were the rest of the Nazgûl finally destroyed?

19. Sauron

1. What caused the War of the Elves and Sauron?
2. What was the name of Sauron's fortress and where was it?
3. Of what people was Sauron?
4. In the downfall of Númenor, what happened to Sauron?
5. How did Sauron bend Saruman's will to his own?
6. After the first thousand years of the Third Age Sauron hid his true identity and worked his evil under what name?
7. In the First Age, Sauron captured Beren, son of Barahir, and cast him into the dungeons of Tol-in-Gaurhoth. Who was it that battled Sauron to rescue him?
8. In Second Age 3262, Ar-Pharazôn, King of Númenor, brought his armies against those of Sauron and commanded Sauron to swear allegiance to him. What did Sauron do?
9. Sauron used his cunning to convince the people of Númenor that the Valar were withholding something from them. What?
10. Who was Sauron's master in the First Age?

20. Spouses

Match each person with his or her spouse.

1. Galadriel
2. Faramir
3. Arwen
4. Beren
5. Manwë
6. Melian
7. Elwing
8. Elrond
9. Lothíriel
10. Oromë

a. Vána
b. Celeborn
c. Eärendil
d. Éomer
e. Éowyn
f. Lúthien
g. Varda
h. Celebrían
i. Thingol
j. Aragorn

21. Types of Peoples

Match the description to the people.

1. Six feet tall, slender, graceful but strong, keen sense of hearing and sight.
2. Four and one-half to five feet tall, broad, strong, and hardy. Very proud.
3. Tall, dark-skinned, black hair and eyes, bright clothing and ornaments.
4. Tall, blond, fair of face, strong even into old age, best horsemen.
5. Tall, dark hair, grey eyes, possessing great wisdom and discernment.
6. Short, squat, bowlegged, long arms, dark faces, squinty eyes, long fangs.
7. Tall, swarthy, dark hair, primitive, uncultured, superstitious.
8. Large, strong, ugly, stupid, turned to stone in the sunlight.
9. The shape of Old Men, great powers controlled by staffs, each had a color.
10. Small, good-natured, leathery feet, sharp-eyed, quick to laugh, hospitable.

a. Dúnedain
b. Dunlendings
c. Dwarves
d. Elves
e. Haradrim
f. Hobbits
g. Orcs
h. Rohirrim
i. Trolls
j. Wizards

22. The Valar

1. Who were the Valar?
2. Name the two greatest Valar.
3. One of the Maiar (lesser Valar) married an Elven king. Who was she and who was he?
4. Which of the Valar was the first victim of Evil?
5. The evil Vala committed an act that brought the wrath of the Noldorin Elves upon him. What did he do?
6. The Valar sent messengers to Middle-earth to work against Evil, but without their awesome powers. What people were the messengers?
7. Where did most of the Valar dwell?
8. Only one Vala came frequently to Middle-earth. Who?
9. The policy of the Valar was to act directly as little as possible but to assist the Free People in their struggle against Evil in what way?
10. The two greatest Valar dwelt where?

23. More on the Valar

Match each Vala with his or her specialty.

1. Manwë
2. Ulmo
3. Aulë
4. Mandos
5. Varda
6. Lórien
7. Tulkas
8. Yavanna
9. Nienna
10. Oromë
11. Vairë
12. Nessa
13. Vána
14. Estë

a. Lord of Waters
b. Giver of Fruits
c. Lady of pity and mourning
d. Lord of Arda, Lord of the Winds
e. Master of visions and dreams
f. The Everyoung
g. Fleetfooted
h. Lady of the Stars
i. The Hunter
j. Rest
k. Greatest in strength
l. Lord of the substance of Arda
m. The Weaver
n. Keeper of the Houses of the Dead

PLACES

1. Inns

1. What was the name of the inn on the Bywater road where the Gaffer told his tales?
2. Which inn had the best beer in Eastfarthing?
3. What was the name of the inn where the hobbits stayed in Bree?
4. What was the name of the inn in Frogmorton that was closed down by Sharkey's Men?
5. What was the name of the inn in Bywater outside of which half a dozen Men waited to waylay the four hobbits?
6. What was the name of the inn on Great East Road by the Brandywine Bridge?
7. What inn was one journey east of Bree on the Great East Road? No one had measured the road past this inn.
8. Which inn did Barliman Butterbur run?
9. In which inn's common-room did Frodo pull his startling disappearing act?
10. At what inn did Thorin Oakenshield await Bilbo on the day of their departure?

2. Forests

1. From what forest did Eärendil get the wood for his boat in which he sailed the Sea?
2. What was the Watchwood?
3. What was the name of the forest between the rivers Teiglin and Sirion?
4. Which forest did the Ents live in and who was it named after?
5. What was the name of the great forest east of the river Anduin before the shadow befell it?
6. The forest in question 5 was renamed after evil overcame it and then again when it was cleansed. What were these names?
7. Name the dense forest forming the south of Doriath.
8. What was the name of the forest east of the river Celon where Elwë (Thingol) met Melian?
9. King Elessar gave a forest in Anórien to a group of people in return for aid during the War of the Ring. Which forest and to whom was it given?
10. East of Buckland was an unfriendly forest where the trees did not like strangers. What was it called?

3. Moria

1. What was the dwarvish name for Moria?
2. What was the name of the stream that the only road to Moria followed long ago?
3. What word opened the West Gate to Moria?
4. What valuable material could be found only in Moria?
5. What creature did the Dwarves uncover in their digging?
6. The Dwarves left Moria after discovering the creature. Who came to live in Moria after they left?
7. What was the reason for the War that led to the Battle of Azanulbizar at the gate to Moria?
8. Which Dwarf of Thorin and Company later led an expedition to resettle Moria?
9. In what room in Moria was this Dwarf's tomb?
10. What was the name of the spiral stair that led to Durin's Tower?

4. Mountains and Hills

1. Name the three mountains that Khazad-dûm lay under.
2. What two mountain ranges formed a wall around Mordor?
3. Name the easternmost peak of the White Mountains where Aragorn found the White Tree sapling.
4. Which mountain was the Gate of the Dead in?
5. What was the name of the mountain east of Mirkwood where the Dwarves lived until Smaug took it over?
6. What was the name of the mountain in Mordor where the One Ring was forged?
7. Name the mountains on which the Seat of Seeing and the Seat of Hearing were built.
8. On what hill in Lothlórien did Aragorn and Arwen plight their troth? It was covered with elanor and niphredil.
9. Which mountain chain ran west from Minas Tirith to the Sea? Dunharrow, Helm's Deep, and the Paths of the Dead were in it.
10. What was the name of the hill that Minas Tirith was built on?

5. Rivers

1. Name the river flowing from Imlad Morgul that had a pale, evil light and smelled noisome.
2. What was the main highway of river traffic between the Men of Lake-town and the Wood-elves of Thranduil's realm in Mirkwood?
3. What river was the natural eastward defense of the Shire?
4. List the seven major rivers of Gondor.
5. What was the chief river of West Beleriand?
6. What was the largest river of Middle-earth?
7. What river was close to the hidden valley of Rivendell and could be made to flood by Elrond to bar the Ford?
8. Anyone who drank of this river or bathed in it fell into a deep sleep. Which river?
9. What river divided East Beleriand from West Beleriand?
10. List the seven rivers of Ossiriand.

6. Towers

1. List the seven beacon-tower hills of Gondor in the order from first to seventh.
2. Name the two Towers of the Teeth.
3. Where were the Towers of the Teeth?
4. What was the name of Sauron's tower at Mordor?
5. In the Second Age, the Army of the Last Alliance destroyed the tower in question, but not its foundations. Why not?
6. What was the name of the tallest of the towers of Emyn Beraid and who was it built for?
7. What was the name of the tower of Isengard?
8. What was the name of the Noldorin tower at Eithel Sirion?
9. What was the name of the "White Horn Tower" at Eglarest?
10. All that was left of the watch-tower on Weathertop at the time of the War of the Ring was an uneven ring of stones. What had been the name of the tower?

OTHERS

1. Animals

1. What was the name of the raven that was Thorin Oakenshield's messenger before the Battle of the Five Armies?
2. Saruman used birds as spies. What kind of birds were they?
3. What were the noble horses that would allow none but the King of Rohan or his sons to ride them?
4. Who was the first of these noble horses?
5. Who was the king of the Eagles of the Misty Mountains during the Battle of the Five Armies?
6. Name the two types of dragons.
7. Which kind was Smaug?
8. What animals were used by the Haradrim as beasts of war?
9. What were the evil wolves of Rhovanion called?
10. What was Draugluin and who killed him?

2. More Animals

1. Who was the greatest of all the Dragons?
2. There was only one way to kill an oliphaunt. How?
3. Who slew Huan, the great wolfhound of Valinor?
4. What were the kine of Araw?
5. What spider had her lair at Cirith Ungol?
6. Who slew Smaug the Golden?
7. Name the ancestor of the Eagles of the Misty Mountains.
8. What birds did the Men of Dale use as messengers?
9. What beast killed Folca, King of Rohan?
10. Ungoliant aided Melkor in destroying the Two Trees of the Valar. Who was she and in what way did she aid him?

3. Battle Quiz

Arrange the following battles in chronological order.

Battle of Azanulbizar
Battle of Dagorlad
Battle of Fornost
Battle of the Camp
Battle of the Crossings of Isen
Battle of the Field of Celebrant
Battle of the Gladden Fields
Battle of the Peak
Battles of the Fords of Isen
Battle of Bywater
Battle of Dale
Battle of Greenfields
Battle of the Crossings of Erui
Battle of the Crossings of Poros
Battle of the Five Armies
Battle of the Hornburg
Battle of the Pelennor Fields

4. More Battles

Match the battle with the two warring factions.

1. Battle of Azanulbizar
2. Battle of Dagorlad
3. Battle of Fornost
4. Battle of Greenfields
5. Battle of the Crossings of Erui
6. Battle of the Field of Celebrant
7. Battle of the Gladden Fields
8. Great Battle
9. Battle of the Peak
10. Battle of the Hornburg

a. Dúnedain vs. the Witch-king
b. Eldacar vs. Castamir
c. Isildur's people vs. Orcs
d. Dunlendings & Orcs vs. Rohirrim
e. Gandalf vs. the Balrog
f. Sauron vs. Last Alliance of Elves
g. Host of Valinor vs. Morgoth
h. Dwarves vs. Orcs
i. Northern Army vs. Balchoth
j. Tooks vs. Orcs

5. Emblems

Match each person or peoples with the insignia used on their banners and shields.

1. Durin and his heirs
2. Eregion
3. Rohan
4. House of Fëanor
5. Sauron
6. Stewards of Gondor
7. Isildur
8. Saruman
9. Kings of Gondor
10. Anárion
11. Minas Morgul
12. Dol Amroth
13. Elendil and his heirs in Gondor
14. Elendil's heirs in Arnor

a. The setting sun
b. White swan ship on a blue field
c. Anvil and hammer under a crown set with seven eight-rayed stars
d. The White Tree, under a silver crown, surrounded by the Seven Stars
e. Holly
f. A rising moon
g. Moon, disfigured by a death's head
h. Seven Stars
i. White hand on black field
j. Eight-rayed silver star
k. Plain white field
l. Red or lidless eye
m. Black field with white tree under seven stars
n. White horse on a green field

6. Horses

Match the horse with its owner or rider.

1. Snowmane
2. Firefoot
3. Roheryn
4. Rochallor
5. Asfaloth
6. Nahar
7. Windfola
8. Felaróf

a. Fingolfin
b. Oromë
c. Éomer
d. Glorfindel
e. King Théoden
f. Aragorn
g. King Eorl
h. Éowyn and Merry

9. Name the greatest horse at the time of the War of the Rings.
10. Who was the sire of Snowmane?

7. Middle-earth Match-up

Match the names with the descriptions.

1. seregon
2. athelas
3. Valaróma
4. palantíri
5. simbelmynë
6. galvorn
7. lembas
8. Arkenstone
9. Nauglamír
10. Sweet Galenas

a. Black, supple, durable metal devised by Eöl, the Dark Elf
b. Gold necklace set with gems from Valinor that gave the wearer grace and loveliness
c. Deep red flower that grew on Amon Rûdh
d. Crystal globes made by the Noldor that showed scenes faraway in space or time
e. A tobacco of Middle-earth
f. Healing plant that grew only where the Númenóreans had camped or lived
g. Delicious, golden meal-cakes baked by the Elves of Lórien
h. Great, white, translucent gem
i. Horn of the Vala Oromë
j. Small white flower that grew on the burial mounds of the Kings of Rohan

8. More Match-ups

Match the names with the descriptions.

1. hithlain
2. miruvor
3. Southlinch
4. elanor
5. mithril
6. ithildin
7. mallos
8. Star of Elendil
9. alfrin
10. silma

a. Light, hard, silver metal found in Khazad-dûm
b. Small, golden flower growing in the fields of Lebennin
c. Tough, light, soft grey substance used in ropes by the Elves of Lórien
d. Crystalline substance shining from within, created by Fëanor
e. Substance made from mithril used in gateways and only visible in starlight or moonlight and after it was touched by one who spoke certain words
f. Clear fragrant cordial of the Eldar
g. Yellow belled spring flower of Lebennin
h. Variety of pipeweed grown in Bree
i. Diamond, heirloom of North-kingdom
j. Yellow, winter, star-shaped flower of Lórien

9. Miscellaneous Match-up

Match each name to its description.

1. Ring of Barahir
2. Ulumúri
3. Horn of the Mark
4. Silver Crown
5. Sceptre of Annúminas
6. Phial of Galadriel
7. niphredil
8. Great Horn
9. cram
10. Silmarils

a. Chief mark of royalty of Arnor
b. Jewels made by Fëanor and containing the light of the Two Trees
c. Travelling food, hard and tasteless
d. Heirloom of the House of Isildur
e. Jar of crystal containing light of Eärendil
f. Chief mark of royalty of Gondor
g. Horns of Ulmo made by the Maia Salmar
h. Heirloom of the House of the Stewards of Gondor
i. Pale winter flower of Lórien
j. Small silver horn made by Dwarves

10. The Palantíri

1. What were the palantíri?
2. Who made them?
3. How many were there?
4. Which palantír looked only to the Undying Lands?
5. Which stone was the master stone?
6. Where was each stone originally kept in Middle-earth?
7. After the year 3019 what would be seen in the stone of Minas Tirith? Why?
8. Which stone did Aragorn claim?
9. Which stone was Sauron believed to control?
10. Who brought the stones to Middle-earth?

11. The Riddle Game

1. What were the stakes in the Riddle-game between Gollum and Bilbo Baggins?

Answer the following riddles:

2. What has roots as nobody sees,
   Is taller than trees,
   Up, up it goes,
   And yet never grows?

3. Thirty white horses on a red hill,
   First they champ,
   Then they stamp,
   Then they stand still.

4. Voiceless it cries,
   Wingless flutters,
   Toothless bites,
   Mouthless mutters.

5. An eye in a blue face
   Saw an eye in a green face.
   "That eye is like to this eye"
   Said the first eye,
   "But in low place,
   Not in high place."

6. It cannot be seen, cannot be felt,
   Cannot be heard, cannot be smelt.
   It lies behind stars and under hills,
   And empty holes it fills.
   It comes first and follows after,
   Ends life, kills laughter.

7. A box without hinges, key, or lid,
   Yet golden treasure inside is hid.

8. Alive without breath,
   As cold as death;
   Never thirsty, ever drinking,
   All in mail never clinking.

9. This thing all things devours:
   Birds, beasts, trees, flowers;
   Gnaws iron, bites steel;
   Grinds hard stones to meal;
   Slays kings, ruins town,
   And beats high mountain down.

10. The last question wasn't technically a riddle, but was accepted as such by Gollum. What was it and what was the answer?
11. Who enforced the rules of the Riddle-game?

12. The Rings

1. There are twenty rings altogether. How many do Mortal Men have?
2. How many do the Elven Lords have?
3. Where are the Elven Lords?
4. The Elven rings each have a name. What are they?
5. The inscription on the One Ring was designed to ensnare all the other rings. It could only be seen when?
6. Who forged the One Ring and where?
7. The One Ring was a plain gold band. What did the others look like?
8. Sauron discovered to his dismay that the rings couldn't dominate the Dwarves by making them evil or lengthening their lives. What did the rings do to their Dwarf bearers?
9. Sauron recovered three of the Dwarves' rings. What happened to the other four?
10. The bearers of the rings of Men were the chief servants of Sauron. What were these invisible beings called?

13. More on the Rings

1. Sauron had a hand in the creation of the Rings of Power excepting for the Three Rings of the Elven Lords. Who forged them and what was their purpose to be?
2. Why weren't the owners of the Three Rings affected by the Ruling Ring?
3. The Rings of Power gave promise of immortality to their wearers. How did this affect the bearers of the Nine?
4. The One Ring created a great desire in others to possess it. Who was it that Frodo offered to give the Ring to, who yet had the strength to refuse it?
5. In Second Age 3434 Sauron lost possession of the One Ring. In what way and at whose hand?
6. The person in question 5 in turn lost possession of it. How?
7. Who were the next two to have possession of the One Ring?
8. What happened to those of little power who wore the Ring?
9. When the One Ring was destroyed, what happened to the other Rings of Power?
10. Although Sauron was of the lesser Valar, in what language was the Ring inscription written?

14. Weapons

1. Sting, Glamdring, and Orcrist were all swords that could warn of the presence of Orcs. How?
2. Orcrist and Glamdring were each called by another name by the Orcs. What were they called?

Match each person with the name of his weapon.

3. Bilbo Baggins
4. Aragorn
5. Gandalf
6. Thorin Oakenshield
7. Fingolfin
8. Gil-galad
9. Elendil
10. Éomer
11. Théoden
12. Lord of the Nazgûls

a. Orcrist
b. Narsil
c. Sting
d. Herugrim
e. Andúril
f. Morgul-Knife
g. Aiglos
h. Glamdring
i. Gúthwinë
j. Ringil

13. Narsil was shattered in battle. It was later reforged into another famous sword. Which one?
14. What other name was Andúril known by?

15. Trees

1. What was the name of the White Tree of the Eldar?
2. There was a tree in Lórien with silver bark and golden leaves. What was it called?
3. What were the names of the Two Trees of the Valar?
4. The Two Trees had a special effect on Valinor. What was it?
5. The casket of the Silver Crown was made from the wood of what tree?
6. What was the Withered Tree?
7. What name was given to the White Tree of Númenor, a descendant of the White Tree of the Eldar?
8. Who poisoned the Two Trees of the Valar?
9. Under what tree did Bilbo make his farewell speech?
10. Lúthien, daughter of King Thingol, was imprisoned at the top of what great beech tree?

16. Who killed _____ ?

1. The Great Goblin?
2. The Lord of the Nazgûl?
3. Smaug the Golden?
4. Azog, king of the Orcs of Khazad-dûm?
5. Bolg, son of Azog?
6. Gandalf the Grey?
7. Uglúk?
8. Saruman?
9. Finwë, King of the Noldor?
10. Fëanor?

Answers

QUESTIONS

1. "His Name Was Baggins"

1. Dwalin, Balin, Kíli, Fíli, Dori, Ori, Óin, Glóin, Bifur, Bofur, Bombur, and Thorin Oakenshield.
2. Tom, Bert, William. They put the Dwarves into sacks while deciding how to eat them.
3. Rune-letters that can only be seen when a moon of the same shape and season as when they were written shines behind them.
4. The first day of the dwarvish New Year, only if the last moon of autumn and the sun are in the sky at the same time.
5. The Eagles of the Misty Mountains.
6. Beorn; a huge black bear.
7. At the very edge of the forest of Mirkwood.
8. Thorin fell asleep upon entering the Wood-elves' circle of light. The Wood-elves then imprisoned him in the king's dungeon.
9. He fell asleep and could not be wakened. The other Dwarves took turns carrying him through the forest for six days until the rain woke him.
10. A great two-handled cup.

2. "Far Over the Misty Mountains Grim"

1. They were looking for a fourteenth member and Gandalf had put a sign at Bilbo's door indicating that Bilbo was a burglar in want of a job.
2. He didn't get Thorin's note until 10:45, leaving him just enough time to run to the Green Dragon Inn to meet them at 11:00.
3. They turn to stone.
4. From the Troll hoard of Bert, William, and Tom.
5. They were captured by Goblins.
6. When he escaped from the Goblin tunnels and came up to their camp unseen.
7. The Wargs and Goblins were going to join forces to attack the villages of Men nearest the mountains.
8. From Beorn, the skin-changer.
9. They saw torches and fires burning in the woods and had hopes of a feast as they were all very hungry.
10. Bilbo put each Dwarf into one of the empty barrels and sent them down the river to Lake-town.

3. "The Mountain Smoked Beneath the Moon"

1. They set fire to the area around the trees that the Dwarves, Bilbo, and Gandalf were in.
2. He told Beorn the story of their escape from the Wargs as the Dwarves showed up two at a time. (Bilbo was first with Gandalf.)
3. Not to drink of or bathe in the stream running through Mirkwood, and never to stray from the path.
4. Eyes, pairs of yellow, red, green, or bulbous eyes.
5. "Stand by the grey stone when the thrush knocks and the setting sun with the last light of Durin's Day will shine upon the key-hole."
6. Elrond.
7. A thrush had heard Bilbo telling the Dwarves of the small spot underneath where Smaug was unprotected, and he flew and told Bard.
8. One-twelfth.
9. The Arkenstone.
10. A horde of Goblins and Wargs attacked them so they joined forces.

4. "To Dungeons Deep and Caverns Old"

1. The Wood-elves and their greatest king, Thranduil.
2. Bilbo Baggins.
3. He was unconscious and invisible.
4. Beorn, he came in bear-shape and was almost giant-sized.
5. Orcrist and the Arkenstone.
6. To repay him for all the food he had eaten while invisible in the King's halls.
7. They were captured by Wood-elves.
8. A coat of mithril-mail, a belt of pearls and crystals, and a leather helm studded with white gems.
9. His cousin Dáin from the Iron Hills.
10. He sent the ravens to deliver the message.

QUOTATIONS

1. "Cheat the Goblins of Their Sport!"

1. Bilbo Baggins, upon being safely deposited in the Eagle's eyrie after rescue from the Wargs and Goblins.
2. William the Troll, after discovering Bilbo trying to pick his pocket.
3. The Lord of the Eagles, on being asked by Gandalf to carry Thorin and Company to a settlement of Men.
4. Balin the Dwarf, when Bilbo appeared out of nowhere after escaping from the Goblins.
5. One of the great spiders of Mirkwood, on the capturing of the Dwarves of Thorin's Company.
6. Bard, just before killing the dragon Smaug.
7. The Great Goblin to Thorin Oakenshield, after finding the Company on their front porch.
8. Thorin Oakenshield to Bilbo Baggins upon learning that Bilbo had given the Arkenstone to Bard.
9. Bilbo, to the spiders of Mirkwood, trying to distract their attention from the Dwarves.
10. Fíli, to the captain of the guards of Lake-town.

2. "Something Strange Is Happening"

1. Bilbo Baggins, to Gandalf the Grey, who was looking for an adventurer.
2. Dori, to Gandalf, on losing Bilbo.
3. Beorn, to Gandalf, on hearing the tale of their encounter with the Wargs.
4. Bilbo, to Balin, as he releases him from the Wood-elves' dungeon.
5. In the Wood-elves' cave, the king's butler to the chief of the guards.
6. Fíli, to Bilbo, after being released from a barrel used to escape from the Wood-elves.
7. Bombur, when the others wanted him to climb up to a higher camp on Lonely Mountain.
8. Thorin, at seeing many birds wheeling around Lonely Mountain.
9. A banner-bearer from the camp of Esgaroth and the Wood-elves, to Thorin at his refusal to parley.
10. Thorin, to Bilbo, just before Thorin died.

TRIVIA

1. "Lazy Lob and Crazy Cob"

1. It gave them deep and pleasant dreams.
2. Galion.
3. Great snails that crawled along the sides of a grey stone in the grass.
4. A crescent moon on a midsummer's eve.
5. Each had a thrice-forged head and a shaft inlaid with cunning gold.
6. Dark green.
7. Black and red.
8. June the twenty-second.
9. The necklace of Girion, made of five hundred emeralds.
10. A harp.

QUESTIONS

1. "The One Ring to Rule Them All"

1. By casting it into the furnace where it was made, in Mordor.
2. Legolas the Elf, Gimli the Dwarf, Gandalf the Grey, Aragorn (or Strider), Boromir of Gondor, Peregrin (Pippin) Took, Samwise (Sam) Gamgee, and Meriadoc (Merry) Brandybuck.
3. He disappeared in a flash of light, compliments of the One Ring and Gandalf the Grey.
4. My precious, Gollum's name for it.
5. The Ring was trying to get back to Sauron, its master.
6. Gandalf caught him listening outside Frodo's window when they were discussing the perils of the Ring. As a "punishment" he agreed Sam should go along.
7. Frodo was compelled to put on the Ring and under its influence he saw the white faces of the Black Riders, their long grey robes, silver helms, and haggard hands holding steel swords.
8. Frodo was wearing the coat of mithril-mail given to Bilbo by Thorin Oakenshield.
9. To Sam she gave a box of earth from her orchard with her blessing on it. To Frodo she gave a phial of the light of Eärendil's star caught in the water of the fountain that filled the Mirror of Galadriel.
10. Strider found it but as the sun rose the blade melted and vanished, leaving only the hilt.

2. "But What About This Frodo?"

1. Ninety-nine.
2. They drowned in the Brandywine River.
3. Thin and stretched.
4. Otho Sacksville-Baggins.
5. Nine years.
6. It did not always seem to be the same size or weight and might slip off a finger where it had been tight.
7. He fades, and eventually becomes permanently invisible.
8. Bilbo.
9. He found that he had put it back into his pocket.
10. It would break his mind.

3. "Well, Now We're Off at Last!"

1. His fiftieth birthday.
2. To Rivendell.
3. Lobelia Sacksville-Baggins.
4. To live in Buckland among his Brandybuck relations.
5. A Black Rider.
6. A band of Elves including Gildor Inglorion.
7. When Frodo was a lad he was caught stealing Farmer Maggot's mushrooms. Farmer Maggot told his dogs that the next time they saw Frodo they could eat him and then the dogs chased Frodo all the way to the Ferry.
8. A thick, tall hedge; the High Hay.
9. Pippin was swallowed up through a crack in the tree and was trapped inside. Merry was trapped in a crack with his legs outside and the rest of him inside the tree.
10. Sam wanted to hurt or frighten the tree by setting fire to it. The tree told Merry that it would squeeze him in two if Sam didn't stop.

4. "There's Something Funny about All This"

1. A Black Rider; he was looking for Frodo.
2. He sang into the crack where Merry was caught and then he hit the willow with a branch.
3. The Barrows.
4. Barrow-wights.
5. He grabbed a short sword and sawed off the hand.
6. Tom Bombadil.
7. Mr. Underhill.
8. He leaped into the air and fell and disappeared.
9. The message told Frodo to leave the Shire no later than the end of July and to get help from Strider; three months before.
10. He was overcome by the Black Breath.

5. "There Were Mysterious Wanderers"

1. Bill Ferny; twelve silver pennies.
2. Glorfindel.
3. His tongue cleaved to his mouth and his sword broke.
4. The river Bruinen rose up and carried them away. (Glorfindel caused the horses of those who weren't in the water to rush into it and also be carried away.)
5. Glóin; Balin, Ori, and Óin had gone to Khazad-dûm and now were not heard from; to seek Elrond's advice and to warn that a messenger from Mordor had tried to enlist Dáin's aid in recovering the Ring from Frodo.
6. The Nazgûl were abroad in the guise of Black Riders and were seeking news of the Shire.
7. Gwaihir the Windlord came looking for Gandalf to deliver a message and carried him away.
8. A flock of large crows flew over, apparently spying out the land.
9. A blizzard of snow came (the ill-will of Caradhras) and forced them to turn back.
10. The path that led through Moria.

6. "Down into the Land of Shadow"

1. Soft footsteps.
2. Orcs, black Uruks, and a Cave-troll.
3. The Elves tied ropes across the river, one for walking on and one to use as a handhold.
4. Each felt that he had been given a choice between the dreaded journey ahead and something he greatly desired.
5. Gollum.
6. They were attacked by Orcs.
7. To go east, alone.
8. The Eye, searching for him.
9. Give the Ring to him to use in defending Minas Tirith.
10. He saw one of the boats seemingly sliding down the bank to the river by itself.

QUOTATIONS

1. "Servant of the Secret Fire"

1. Glorfindel, to Frodo, when he wouldn't leave on the Elf's horse for the house of Elrond.
2. Gandalf, to Balrog, on the Bridge of Khazad-dûm.
3. Legolas, at being blindfolded along with all the others of the Fellowship to be led through Lórien.
4. Boromir, to Frodo at Amon Hen.
5. Rory Brandybuck at Bilbo's birthday party.
6. A fox, passing the woods where Frodo slept on his first day out of the Shire.
7. Elrond, to Frodo, prior to their departure from his house.
8. Bilbo, to Frodo, after giving him the coat of mithril-mail to wear under his clothing.
9. Aragorn, of Frodo, at Amon Hen as the Fellowship decides whether to go to Minas Tirith or east to the Shadow.
10. Tom Bombadil, to Frodo, as Frodo tried to use the Ring to sneak out of the room.

2. "You . . . You're a Brandybuck!"

1. Bilbo, to Gandalf, at giving up the Ring to Frodo.
2. Lobelia Sackville-Baggins to Frodo, at being escorted out of Bag End after Bilbo's estate was settled.
3. Gandalf, to Frodo, about letting Gollum live.
4. Sam Gamgee, to Frodo, when Gandalf caught him eavesdropping.
5. Gildor Inglorion, to Frodo, while sitting in the forest near Woodhall.
6. Frodo, to Pippin, at seeing a Black Rider while they were in the thicket south of Woodhall.
7. Tom Bombadil, to Frodo, about Farmer Maggot.
8. Tom Bombadil, as he gave each of the four hobbits a knife from the Barrow-wight's treasure.
9. Frodo, as they prepared to make camp at Weathertop.
10. Gandalf, to Saruman, when he declared himself the Many-Coloured.

3. "Power of the Dark Lord!"

1. Gandalf, to Elrond, on including Merry and Pippin in the Company of the Ring.
2. Elrond, to the Company of the Ring on their departure.
3. Aragorn, to Gandalf and Gimli, about taking a path through Moria.
4. Aragorn, to Sam, after they escaped from Moria.
5. Boromir, to Aragorn, on entering Lothlórien.
6. Haldir, to Legolas, on blindfolding the Company to journey through Lothlórien.
7. Gimli, to Galadriel, when she asked him to name a gift.
8. Gandalf, to the Company, on closing the door to a passage of Moria.
9. Galadriel, to Frodo, shortly after he offered her the Ring.
10. Strider, to Pippin, on discovering the Trolls of stone from Bilbo's adventure.

TRIVIA

1. "The World Was Fair"

1. A dozen bottles of Old Winyards.
2. Seven, in red ink.
3. A spotted toad in a garden full of grass-snakes.
4. One hundred years old.
5. About three hours.
6. Number 3 Bagshot Row.
7. A basket of mushrooms.
8. The sound of the Sea far-off.
9. The Withywindle valley.
10. A brooch set with blue stones.

2. "The Mountains Tall"

1. Sharp-ears, Wise-nose, Swish-tail, Bumpkin, and White-socks.
2. Apples.
3. "Oh Elbereth! Githoniel!"
4. Four nights and three days.
5. "Naur an edraith ammen!"
6. A great red sword and a whip of many thongs.
7. South-west.
8. Thirty-eight years.
9. Galadriel.
10. Galadriel herself and her maidens.

1. "The Orcs Were Getting Ready"

1. Some of the Orcs were not from Mordor but bore Saruman's emblem and they could endure the Sun.
2. He, Legolas, and Gimli laid Boromir in one of the elven boats and sent it down the Anduin.
3. The leaf-brooch from his elven cloak.
4. Because of their elven-cloaks.
5. Éomer, Third Marshal of the Riddermark.
6. Grishnákh.
7. Wellinghall; two vessels filled with a clear liquid that glowed with golden and with green light when Fangorn held his hands over them.
8. He and his Orcs were cutting down trees in great numbers.
9. Gandalf the White.
10. Nazgûl, mounted on winged steeds.

2. "The King of the Golden Hall"

1. He believed trouble followed Gandalf "like crows," and also Gandalf had taken Shadowfax and now no other could ride him.
2. Gandalf cast Wormtongue to the floor, speechless, and took Théoden outside where he again stood tall and knew his own counsel.
3. The ownership of Shadowfax.
4. Éomer; Éowyn.
5. Helm's Deep.
6. A great forest stood where no trees had been.
7. Gandalf, and Erkenbrand and his men.
8. Saruman had told them that the Rohirrim burned their captives alive.
9. Treebeard and the Ents, and Merry and Pippin.
10. Huorns.

3. Flotsam and Jetsam

1. They flooded the circle of Isengard around Orthanc, putting out the fires underneath it.
2. Treebeard sent him swimming across the waters to Orthanc.
3. He sent Huorns to help.
4. His words seemed wise and reasonable and made others who spoke seem harsh and uncouth.
5. The Key of Orthanc, and his staff.
6. The palantír of Orthanc.
7. Treebeard and the Ents.
8. He stole the palantír from Gandalf and looked into it.
9. Sauron saw him and he became rigid and unseeing.
10. A winged Nazgûl.

4. Past the Marshes, Beyond the Black Gate

1. The rope came tumbling down after them.
2. Frodo said the knot came loose. Sam said the rope came when he called it.
3. He began screaming in pain and biting at the knot.
4. It seemed to freeze him, to bite into his leg; because it was an Elven rope.
5. Gollum-Sméagol swore to serve the master of "the Precious."
6. Faces, dead faces.
7. He held a debate with himself as to whether or not he should steal "the Precious."
8. Rabbits; he made stew.
9. They saw the smoke from Sam's fire.
10. An oliphaunt.

5. "An Evil Thing in Spider-form"

1. The Men of Harad.
2. He was Boromir's younger brother.
3. Henneth Annûn; a great waterfall.
4. Of wizards, of Gandalf.
5. Calenardhon.
6. He was leading a great army out of Minas Morgul.
7. The phial of Galadriel.
8. Shelob, the Great Spider.
9. A gigantic cobweb; the elvish blade Sting cut through it.
10. Gollum.
11. Whether to stay with Frodo's body or to take the Ring and go on.
12. That he wasn't dead.

QUOTATIONS

1. "There Is Evil Afoot"

1. Aragorn, on discovering Orcs wearing Saruman's emblem.
2. Éomer, to Aragorn, at their first meeting.
3. Grishnákh, to Merry and Pippin, at the edge of Fangorn Forest.
4. Fangorn, to Merry and Pippin, talking about Saruman.
5. Aragorn, to Gandalf, after meeting him in Fangorn Forest.
6. Gwaihir the Windlord, to Gandalf, on rescuing him from the top of Celebdil.
7. Wormtongue, to Gandalf, at Meduseld.
8. Gandalf, to Wormtongue, at Meduseld.
9. Théoden, to Gandalf, to repay him for exposing Wormtongue.
10. Gandalf, to Aragorn, about going after Merry and Pippin.

2. "An Old Liar with Honey on His Forked Tongue?"

1. Erkenbrand, to the hillmen, after their capture.
2. Legolas, to Merry and Pippin, at Isengard.
3. Aragorn at Isengard, speaking of Wormtongue.
4. Éomer, to Théoden, about Saruman.
5. Saruman, to Gandalf, when he asked for Saruman's staff as a pledge of conduct to be returned later.
6. Merry, to Pippin, about Gandalf.
7. Samwise, to Frodo, on leaving the elf-rope tied to a stump.
8. Frodo, to Gollum, who was squeezing Sam.
9. Faramir, to Mablung and Damrod, about blindfolding Frodo and Sam.
10. Faramir, to Frodo, after Sam blurted out what Isildur's Bane was.

TRIVIA

1. "The Window on the West"

1. Forty leagues and five.
2. Hasufel; Gárulf.
3. Two evergreen trees.
4. Fangorn, Finglas, and Fladrif (Treebeard, Leaflock, and Skinbark).
5. Láthspell (Ill-news).
6. Twenty feet high.
7. Nine days.
8. 1417.
9. Until seven times the years that Saruman tormented the Ents had passed.
10. Eighteen fathoms, or thirty ells.

2. Perils of the Journey

1. A foul sump of oily many-coloured ooze.
2. Swertings.
3. King Eärnur.
4. Mablung and Damrod.
5. Green.
6. Wood from the fair tree lebethron.
7. The Straight Stair and the Winding Stair.
8. Torech Ungol.
9. Ufthak.
10. He hewed off one of her claws.

QUESTIONS

1. "Seven Stars, Seven Stones, One White Tree"
1. Seven.
2. His service and his sword.
3. Check on Shadowfax.
4. Prince of the Halflings.
5. Thirty Rangers of the North and Elrond's sons.
6. "The days are short. If thou art in haste, remember the Paths of the Dead."
7. He looked into the Stone of Orthanc.
8. Their king swore allegiance to Isildur but refused to aid him against Sauron.
9. That he would be the last king and he and his people would never rest until the oath was fulfilled.
10. He summoned the Dead to fulfill their oath.

2. "Ride Now, Ride Now! Ride to Gondor!"
1. The Red Arrow, a black-feathered arrow with point painted red.
2. The sky was covered with a great gloom that would let no sunlight through. As it came from Mordor it was taken as the beginning of war.
3. That she arm Merry for battle.
4. Dernhelm.
5. Five winged Nazgûl; Gandalf the White.
6. The One Ring.
7. Missiles that burst into flame, and the heads of those who had died in the battles before.
8. Denethor refused to leave Faramir, who had been stricken ill.
9. Gandalf, and the Prince of Dol Amroth and his knights.
10. He had Faramir taken to the tombs and ordered himself and Faramir burned.

3. "Lord of the Black Land Come Forth!"

1. The Gate.
2. The Woses', Wild Men of the Wood.
3. He offered to show them a road to Minas Tirith that wasn't blocked by Orcs.
4. For them to leave the Wild Men alone and not hunt them like beasts.
5. The headless bodies of two errand-riders of Gondor headed for Gondor, one clasping the red arrow.
6. It blew away the darkness, bringing the dawn.
7. Dernhelm, or Éowyn.
8. They were either lying slain about him or carried far away by the madness of their horses.
9. He was killed by a hobbit and a woman.
10. Snowmane was stricken by a black dart and in his fall crushed Théoden.

4. "War Now Calls Us!"

1. Aragorn and many allies.
2. Beregond.
3. When Denethor used the palantír Sauron controlled what he saw.
4. His right arm was useless and cold and he had the Black Breath.
5. He healed those who had been hurt and it proved that he was their king.
6. Fear; they filled the enemies with the madness of terror.
7. A wind blew up from the Sea.
8. To draw Sauron's attention away from Mordor, to help the Ring-bearer.
9. He will believe that one of them is the new Ringlord.
10. To leave, to go to Cair Andros and recapture it.

5. "Towers Strong and High"

1. The Mouth of Sauron; the Lieutenant of the Tower of Barad-dûr.
2. The messenger finally quailed as though physically threatened.
3. Sam's sword, a grey elven cloak with brooch, and Frodo's coat of mithril-mail.
4. Many hosts of enemy that had been hidden surrounded the Army of the West.
5. He stabbed a great Hill-troll that was attacking Beregond and it fell upon him.
6. The Eagles were coming.
7. To keep enemies *in* Mordor.
8. He used the phial of Galadriel to crumble their will.
9. They let out a shrill cry of alarm.
10. The companies led by Shagrat and Gorbag killed each other off over Frodo's belongings.

6. "The Crack of Doom"

1. It crumbled and fell.
2. One of the winged Nazgûl.
3. Clean water and plain daylight.
4. Apparently so; the darkness cleared and they found a trickle of water.
5. A troop of Orcs came by and they were forced to march with them. (They were mistaken for deserting Orcs.)
6. More troops of Orcs came along and were jostling for position and they escaped unnoticed.
7. Sam carried Frodo on his back.
8. Gollum.
9. He claimed the Ring as his own and put it on.
10. He became aware of it and was fearful; all else was forgotten as he sent his Nazgûl hurrying to Mount Doom.

7. "The Ring-bearer Has Fulfilled His Quest"

1. Gollum fought with Frodo, bit off his finger, and then fell into the chasm.
2. Gandalf and the Eagles (Gwaihir, Landroval, Meneldor) came for them and bore them away.
3. March 25th, the day Sauron fell.
4. The clothes they wore to Mordor, even the Orc-rags.
5. Gimli; he saw a hobbit foot under a heap of bodies.
6. Faramir; Frodo; and Gandalf.
7. He sent him out of Minas Tirith — as Captain of the Guard of Faramir.
8. The day when he and Arwen Evenstar were wed; Midsummer's Day.
9. A sapling of the White Tree.
10. Go over the Sea into the West.

8. Partings

1. A small silver horn engraved with horsemen.
2. At the Treegarth of Orthanc; Isengard.
3. To Fangorn Forest; Legolas had agreed to go to the Glittering Caves at Helm's Deep if Gimli would go in turn to Fangorn Forest.
4. Saruman and Wormtongue.
5. Bilbo's one hundred and twenty-ninth birthday.
6. He kept falling asleep.
7. To Frodo he regave the mithril-mail and Sting, and three books he had written; to Sam he gave a small bag of gold; to Merry and Pippin each he gave an elf-made pipe decorated with silver and pearl.
8. To see Tom Bombadil.
9. Bill Ferny.
10. To leave the Shire and never return.

9. Trouble at the Shire

1. A band of Shirriffs; to put the four hobbits under arrest.
2. They laughed.
3. They were used to bullying helpless hobbits, not fearless warriors with weapons.
4. He blew the horn of Rohan.
5. Rosie Cotton.
6. Lotho Sacksville-Baggins; to help him keep power over the Shire.
7. Saruman.
8. To get even with the four hobbits for his downfall.
9. That Frodo would have neither health nor long life.
10. To help hobbits made homeless by the troubles.

10. "The End of Fellowship in the Middle-earth"

1. He reduced the Shirriffs to their former number and function.
2. He planted saplings to replace the felled trees and put a grain of the sand at the roots of each. The silver nut he planted at the Party Tree site. The rest of the sand he threw to the winds.
3. All the saplings grew very fast. The silver nut yielded a mallorn tree.
4. His Morgul-wound pained him; he sickened from Shelob's bite.
5. Elanor, the sun-star.
6. To the Havens, to go over the Sea.
7. Círdan the Shipwright, and Gandalf.
8. The Three Rings; Vilya, Nenya, and Narya.
9. Merry and Pippin.
10. All his belongings.

QUOTATIONS

1. "We Must Ride Our Own Road"

1. Denethor, to Gandalf, of his son Boromir's death.
2. Beregond telling Pippin about Faramir.
3. Pippin, to Beregond, about the coming battle with Mordor.
4. Aragorn, to Théoden, at their parting.
5. Merry, to King Théoden, when he spoke of leaving Merry behind.
6. Denethor, to Faramir, when he learned Faramir had had opportunity to seize the Ring.
7. Denethor, before he and Faramir were taken to the tombs.
8. Lord of the Nazgûl, to Gandalf, at the Gate to Minas Tirith.
9. Pippin, warning Beregond of Denethor's plans to kill Faramir.
10. Merry, to Elfhelm, after Elfhelm tripped over him.

2. "The Houses of Lamentation"

1. Lord of the Nazgûl's threat to Dernhelm-Éowyn, as she protected Théoden.
2. Éowyn's reply to the Lord of the Nazgûl.
3. Éomer, to Aragorn, as he came to war at Minas Tirith.
4. Denethor, as Beregond prevents him from stabbing Faramir, to Gandalf.
5. Merry, on awaking from the Black Breath, to Aragorn.
6. Ioreth, speaking of the athelas, or kingsfoil.
7. Gimli, to Legolas, speaking of the differences in the quality of the stonework, at Minas Tirith.
8. Legolas, on the awakening of the sea-longing, to Gimli, Merry, and Pippin.
9. Gandalf, to the captains of Gondor, proposing an attack upon Sauron.
10. Prince Imrahil, at the council of captains, on the impossibility of a victory.

3. "A Piece of Elvish Glass"

1. The Mouth of Sauron, to Aragorn, at the Black Gate.
2. Gandalf, to the Mouth of Sauron, in reply.
3. Sam, to himself, on the last stages of their journey to Mount Doom.
4. Gandalf, asking Gwaihir the Windlord to carry him to find Frodo.
5. Sam, to Gandalf, on awakening in Ithilien.
6. Aragorn, instructing Faramir on Minas Ithil.
7. Gandalf, in answer to Frodo's questions about the day Aragorn awaits.
8. Gandalf, to Aragorn, who wished him to stay as counsel.
9. Gimli, to King Éomer, on their debate over Lady Galadriel.
10. Éomer, to Aragorn, at their meeting after Aragorn is crowned King.

4. "Go in Peace!"

1. Gandalf, to Treebeard, on hearing he had let Saruman loose.
2. Treebeard, to Celeborn and Galadriel, at their parting.
3. Saruman, to Merry, who gave him some of the tobacco found in Isengard.
4. Frodo, to Gandalf, speaking of the recurrent pain from the Morgul-wound.
5. Gandalf, to the four hobbits, about their going to the Shire without him.
6. Merry, to the other three hobbits, after Gandalf leaves.
7. Frodo, in answer to the Shirriff's claim that he was under arrest.
8. Frodo, to Sam, when he wanted to kill Saruman.
9. Frodo, explaining to Sam why he was going over the Sea.
10. Gandalf, to Merry, Pippin, and Sam, as the ship prepared to leave.

TRIVIA

1. The Sounds of War
1. Rammas Echor.
2. Four years.
3. Third Company of the Citadel.
4. Black with no visible device.
5. Hirgon.
6. Fen Hollen.
7. Grond.
8. In memory of the Hammer of the Underworld.
9. Shadowfax.
10. The Púkel-men of Dunharrow.

2. Who and What
1. Guthláf.
2. Black serpent upon scarlet.
3. Faramir—fragrance of dewy mornings in a land more fair than any now known. Éowyn—a fresh clean scentless air, as though new made from snowy mountains. Merry—scent of orchards and heather in sunshine.
4. Fifty.
5. Mablung.
6. Snaga.
7. Shagrat.
8. Elbereth.
9. The fourteenth of the New Year; April eighth, Shire Reckoning.
10. A white, star-shaped gem on a silver chain.

APPENDICES

A–I. Kingdoms of the Middle-earth

1. Arnor, the North-kingdom, and Gondor to the South.
2. Elendil.
3. A seedling of Nimloth, and the Seven Seeing-stones.
4. Arthedain.
5. The Lossoth, the Snowmen of Forochel.
6. The Witch-king, or the Lord of the Nazgûl.
7. It was crushed by ice and Arvedui drowned.
8. By the Chieftains of the Dúnedain.
9. The ring of Barahir, the shards of Narsil, the star of Elendil, and the sceptre of Annúminas.
10. King Valacar wed a woman of the lesser Men, not a Dúnedain. Many refused to accept her son when he succeeded to the throne.

A–II. Notes from a Loremaster's Journal

1. Castamir, the Captain of Ships.
2. At Umbar.
3. A great plague came out of the East.
4. The Wainriders.
5. Eärnil, distant relation to the dead king.
6. Arvedui, heir of the North-kingdom.
7. As the Witch-king advanced upon Eärnur his horse bolted and before he got it under control the Witch-king had fled.
8. He went to Minas Morgul on a challenge from the Witch-king and was never heard of again.
9. Mardil the Steward.
10. The Ruling Stewards, of the House of Húrin.

A–III. Who, What, and When

1. Beren.
2. The White Tree.
3. Thorongil recommended relying on Gandalf; Denethor's trust was in Saruman.
4. Arathorn and Gilraen.
5. Mansbane threw Eorl's father, Léod, and killed him and thus owed Eorl a great weregild.
6. The marriage of Helm's daughter to Freca's son Wulf.
7. Wulf.
8. He believed that if he bore no weapons, no weapon could bite on him.
9. Thengel and Morwen of Lossarnach in Gondor.
10. The gift of Cirion, giving Rohan to the Eorlingas; the Oath of Eorl, pledging aid to Gondor.

B. Legends of the Ages

1. The Great Battle in which Morgoth was overthrown.
2. The overthrow of Sauron and the taking of the One Ring.
3. The Third Age ended with the end of the War of the Ring, with the passing of Saruman; the Fourth Age began when Elrond departed Middle-earth (in Gondor it was reckoned in March instead).
4. The Star of the Dúnedain.
5. Over the Sea, as the last Ring-bearer.
6. The Red Book given to him by Frodo.
7. King Éomer in Edoras.
8. Peregrin Took.
9. Meriadoc's and Peregrin's.
10. Gimli the Dwarf.

QUESTIONS

1. "The Beginning of Days"

1. Varda, Lady of the Stars.
2. Yavanna.
3. Elves and Men; Elves.
4. Melkor; he wanted Arda for his own and the Valar resisted.
5. Aulë was impatient for someone to whom he could teach his crafts.
6. The trees; the Shepherds of the Trees, the Ents.
7. He was chained and cast into the fastness of Mandos.
8. The Eldar.
9. He played music for them on his horns of shell.
10. It was on their behalf that the Valar had gone to war with Melkor, resulting in his downfall.

2. "The Darkening"

1. After his sentence was over Melkor put on such a convincing show of repentance that he was released.
2. It became scorched and withered.
3. He was banished from the elven city, Tirion, for twelve years.
4. No.
5. The Balrogs.
6. He set them in a crown of iron and wore it always.
7. They vowed to pursue with vengeance and hatred to the ends of the World anyone who tried to keep a Silmaril from them.
8. The Teleri refused to give their ships to the Noldor so the Noldor took them by force.
9. Finarfin.
10. When the Noldor came to the strait of Helcaraxë, Fëanor and his sons took the few ships and crossed, leaving Fingolfin's followers stranded in the cold. Fëanor then burned the ships.

3. Lore of the Ancients

1. Menegroth, the Thousand Caves.
2. Orcs.
3. An unseen wall of shadow and bewilderment that none could pass against Melian's will or the will of King Thingol (unless possessing a power greater than Melian's).
4. The Sun was made of the last golden fruit of Laurelin; the Moon of the last silver flower of Telperion.
5. The Noldor under Fëanor, and the Orcs of Angband.
6. Fingon cut his hand off.
7. A helm, mail, and a sword; so that Turgon would recognize the one who came from Nevrast to warn him of the peril of fire.
8. Finrod Felagund.
9. Morgoth, or one of his servants, used Amlach's form to speak at the council of Men.
10. His ring.

4. "The Hidden King"

1. Fingolfin.
2. Thorondor, King of Eagles.
3. They were lost after battling Orcs and Thorondor sent two eagles to rescue them. They were taken to Gondolin.
4. He tricked Gorlim into believing he saw his missing wife, causing him to cry out and make his presence known.
5. Barahir's hiding place in Dorthonion.
6. The birds and beasts of Dorthonion aided him and in return he ate no meat.
7. A Silmaril.
8. Finrod Felagund.
9. Celegorm, son of Fëanor; he persuaded her to come to Nargothrond and there imprisoned her.
10. Three times.

5. "Tales of Sorrow"

1. Huan the hound.
2. Finrod Felagund burst his bonds and battled the werewolf until they both died, saving Beren.
3. A mighty werewolf; Huan.
4. Celegorm, son of Fëanor; when Celegorm would have slain Beren Huan stopped him.
5. The light glowed through his flesh but it did not burn him.
6. Carcharoth was not afraid and bit Beren's hand off.
7. The Silmaril burned inside him, causing madness.
8. That he should not meet death until he encountered the mightiest wolf that would ever walk the world.
9. That he wait for her beyond the Western Sea, in the halls of Mandos.
10. She chose to give up her chance to go to Valimar, to dwell instead in Middle-earth with Beren as mortal until they both died.

6. "The Doom Lies in Yourself"

1. Although he and his Men went to battle on the side of the Noldor, they turned and fought for Morgoth.
2. Out of his house would come the hope of Elves and Men—if he lived.
3. To Doriath.
4. On Amon Rûdh.
5. Beleg rescued Túrin—unconscious—from Orcs. When he went to cut Túrin's bonds he pricked him with the sword. Túrin killed him believing him to be an enemy.
6. He became motionless.
7. His sister, unknown to him when they met.
8. She cast herself into the river at the Cabed-en-Aras, a deep gorge.
9. He cast himself upon his sword.
10. The blood of Beleg its master and the unjust slaying of Brandir.

7. Elves and Men

1. Melian the Maia.
2. Nauglamír, Necklace of the Dwarves.
3. He got it in Nargothrond, where he slew Mîm.
4. He wanted the Silmaril mounted in it.
5. When it was finished the Dwarves refused to give it back and slew Thingol for it.
6. The shield, mail, and sword Turgon left behind as Ulmo ordered.
7. Ulmo had commanded Tuor to go to Gondolin. When Voronwë learned of this he agreed to be Tuor's guide.
8. To abandon Gondolin and go to the Sea.
9. Tuor and Idril Celebrindal.
10. Maeglin, son of Eöl.

8. The War of Wrath

1. Lordship of Gondolin and possession of Idril Celebrindal.
2. Idril had ordered a secret way out made.
3. He wanted to plead with the Valar to aid Middle-earth.
4. They were to choose which of Two Kindred they would belong to.
5. To sail the heavens with the Silmaril on his brow, as a sign of hope.
6. They went to war again with Morgoth.
7. He broke the towers of Thangorodrim.
8. Through the Door of Night, into the Timeless Void.
9. It was changed beyond recognition; hills cast down, rivers rerouted, valleys upheaved.
10. One was set into the sky, one was cast into the Sea, and one was cast into a fire at the bottom of a deep chasm.

TRIVIA

1. Elves, Dwarves, and Balrogs

1. Rúmil.
2. Nimphelos
3. Vingilot, the Foam-flower.
4. Seven times.
5. Gorthaur.
6. The Valaraukar.
7. Ten.
8. Ormal and Illuin.
9. Dagor-nuin-Giliath, Battle-under-Stars.
10. Cabed Naeramarth, Leap of Dreadful Doom.

AKALLABÊTH

1. Wisdom, power, a great expanse of life; Númenor.
2. Elros, son of Eärendil.
3. That the Dúnedan could not sail west out of sight of Númenor.
4. The King's Men were estranged from the Eldar and the Valar because they envied the Eldar's immortality; the Faithful remained true to the Lords of the West and kept their friendship with the Elves.
5. Melkor.
6. He went secretly to the courts of the King and stole a fruit from the White Tree.
7. He made ready ships for the Faithful to flee in.
8. Aman was removed beyond the reach of Men.
9. He cast it into the chasm that had swallowed up the Númenórean fleet.
10. Elendil and the Faithful.

PEOPLE — FAIR FRIENDS AND FIERCE FOES

1. Aragorn

1. Strider.
2. The Dúnadan; Man of the West, Númenórean.
3. Two hundred and ten.
4. Rivendell.
5. Estel.
6. King of both Gondor and Anor.
7. Eldarion.
8. The Reunited Kingdom.
9. Thorongil.
10. Telcontar.

2. Bilbo Baggins

1. He was crawling through the dark goblin tunnels and his hand came upon it.
2. He heard Glóin speaking to Gandalf about him. The words "little fellow bobbing on the mat" made him wish to be thought of as fierce. Also he had some Took blood in him.
3. He killed the giant spider that tried to capture him.
4. He clung, invisible, to one of the empty barrels the Elves dumped into the river.
5. He put on the magic ring and vanished from sight.
6. He was struck by a stone from above and knocked unconscious.
7. A small chest of silver and one filled with gold such as a strong pony could carry.
8. They were having an auction to settle his estate.
9. He went to Rivendell.
10. To avoid unpleasant callers.

3. Bilbo's Birthday

1. September 22.
2. Thirty-three.
3. Thursday.
4. Dale.
5. Twelve dozen, or one Gross.
6. Bilbo's age added to Frodo's age equaled one hundred forty-four.
7. It was a mountain out of which flew a red-golden dragon that flew all around the crowd.
8. Golden.
9. Gandalf the Grey.
10. That he was leaving Bag End NOW.

4. Tom Bombadil

1. Goldberry, the daughter of the River.
2. Master of wood, water, and hill.
3. He was looking for water-lilies for Goldberry.
4. It was Goldberry's washing day; she called the rain.
5. To ward off the rain so he wouldn't get wet.
6. The Eldest.
7. Before the river and the trees; before the Elves passed Westward.
8. Farmer Maggot.
9. Nothing! Tom didn't disappear.
10. By Elves he was called Iarwain Ben-adar; by Dwarves, Forn; and Orald by Northern Men.

5. Fair Friends of Fierce Foes
1. Gandalf the Grey.
2. Beorn, the skin-changer.
3. Tom Bombadil.
4. Boromir.
5. Fangorn.
6. Théoden, son of Thengel.
7. Ghân-buri-Ghân, headman of the Woses.

6. Dwarves
1. The Vala Aulë fashioned them. Eru gave them life out of compassion for Aulë.
2. Khazad-dûm.
3. Mithril, a light, hard, silvery metal.
4. The Dragons.
5. Axes.
6. Durin I.
7. Thrain II, King of Durin's Folk in exile.
8. Gimli, one of the Company of the Ring.
9. Khuzdul.
10. Naugrim, "fire people."

7. More Dwarves

1. They were held to be Durin the Deathless returned.
2. In stone.
3. They were burned.
4. Dís.
5. They dressed as men; also they were similar in voice and appearance.
6. Less than one-third.
7. Lord of the Glittering Caves.
8. Mithril and steel.
9. Dáin II Ironfoot.
10. Balin.

8. Elves

1. They rested their minds by thinking of past ages or looking at beautiful things.
2. Growing things, music, and above all the stars.
3. Over the Sea to Eldamar in Valinor.
4. Círdan, of the Eldar.
5. Fëanor.
6. Vanyar, Noldor, and Teleri.
7. Galadriel, Noldorin princess.
8. Galadriel, Círdan, and Gil-galad.
9. Thingol Greycloak.
10. Lúthien, most beautiful Elven-lady of all time.

9. More Elves

1. "Advice is a dangerous gift, even from the wise to the wise."
2. Lúthien Tinúviel.
3. Celeborn, Lord of the Galadrim.
4. Orcs.
5. Elrond.
6. Ingwë, Finwë, and Elwë.
7. A. 3
   B. 5
   C. 1
   D. 2
   E. 4
8. His spirit was so fiery that when it left his body fell to ash.
9. The Moriquendi.
10. The Vanyar.

10. Ents

1. Tree-herders, the most ancient people on Middle-earth.
2. The Entwives were lost so there were no more Entings; also many Ents were becoming treeish.
3. A gathering of Ents, a council; at Derndingle.
4. Trolls.
5. Ents slept standing up; they were nourished by Ent-draughts.
6. A very heavy axe-stroke; also by fire.
7. They compress the work of a tree-root in a hundred years into a few moments and crumble rock.
8. Beechbone.
9. Treegarth of Orthanc.
10. News of the Entwives.

11. Gandalf the Grey

1. Círdan the shipwright; Narya.
2. Olórin.
3. He became Gandalf the White and his power greatly increased.
4. With a thundering incantation he caused a tree to catch fire and it in turn caused a whole circle of trees to catch fire and the wolves fled.
5. Where the One Ring was.
6. He imprisoned Gandalf in Isengard.
7. He put a good word on it (for seven years) when he learned Strider went east with the four hobbits.
8. The Dwarf Thráin; the map and key to Erebor, the Lonely Mountain.
9. He wanted Smaug destroyed before Sauron could use him in war.
10. The Maiar; Nienna, one of the Valier.

12. Gollum

1. Aragorn.
2. He used it to find out secrets.
3. Sméagol; because he muttered and gurgled in his throat.
4. He said his grandmother gave it to him and that she had lots like it.
5. The Land of Mordor.
6. He put him in prison under the Wood-elves' care.
7. He had escaped, aided by Orcs.
8. He crawled down, insect-like, head first.
9. Slinker and Stinker; Slinker for Gollum's fawning manner to Frodo, Stinker when he became hateful and bitter.
10. Shelob, the great spider; he figured he'd get the ring back after Shelob killed Frodo and Sam.

13. Hobbits

1. Their feet grew leathery soles and were covered by thick brown hair.
2. b, e
3. c, d
4. a, f
5. Stoors.
6. Green and yellow.
7. Bilbo Baggins; 131 years and 8 days.
8. Meriadoc Brandybuck and Peregrin Took. Because they drank Ent-draughts given to them by Fangorn.
9. Déagol.
10. Sméagol, or Trahald.

14. More Hobbits

1. Anything a hobbit had no use for but wouldn't throw away.
2. Round.
3. It was a numerous and exceedingly wealthy family.
4. Every seven years.
5. Postmaster, and First Shirriff.
6. Thirty-three.
7. The Sacksville-Baggins family.
8. Gandalf the Grey.
9. The Fallohide branch.
10. Halflings.
11. They were fond of boats and some could swim.

PEOPLE — FAIR FRIENDS AND FIERCE FOES 131

15. Famous Hobbits

1. Bandobras (Bullroarer) Took.
2. Tobold Hornblower of Longbottom.
3. Ham Gamgee; he was the gardener at Bag End.
4. Drogo Baggins and Primula Brandybuck.
5. Marcho and Blanco.
6. Gorhendad Oldbuck.
7. Bucca of the Marish.
8. Elanor Gamgee, daughter of Samwise.
9. Fastred of Greenholm; Mayor Samwise Gamgee.
10. Will Whitfoot, then Mayor of Michel Delving.

16. Names

1. d
2. f
3. e
4. h
5. c
6. a
7. j
8. i
9. g
10. b

17. More Names

1. a, e, h
2. d, k
3. g, l
4. b
5. j, o
6. f, q
7. c
8. p
9. n
10. i
11. m

18. The Nazgûl

1. Nine.
2. They were enslaved by the Nine Rings.
3. Over four thousand years.
4. Angmar.
5. Battle of the Pelennor Fields.
6. To find Frodo and the Ring.
7. On top of Weathertop.
8. Weapons with special spells on them.
9. At night.
10. They were destroyed when the One Ring was cast into Orodruin.

19. Sauron

1. Celebrimbor discovered Sauron's treachery in the forging of the Rings.
2. Barad-dûr, at the southern end of the Ered Lithui.
3. Sauron was of the Maiar, the lesser Valar.
4. His mortal body was destroyed although his spirit lived on.
5. Saruman used the Palantír of Orthanc and was ensnared by Sauron, who had the Palantír of Minas Ithil.
6. The Necromancer, of Dol Guldur.
7. Huan, the wolf-hound; and Lúthien, daughter of Thingol Greycloak and the Maia Melian.
8. Sauron humbled himself before Ar-Pharazôn and allowed himself to be taken back to Númenor as a hostage.
9. Immortality.
10. Melkor, or Morgoth.

20. Spouses

1. b
2. e
3. j
4. f
5. g
6. i
7. c
8. h
9. d
10. a

21. Types of Peoples

1. d
2. c
3. e
4. h
5. a
6. g
7. b
8. i
9. j
10. f

22. The Valar

1. Those of the Ainur (Holy Ones) who came to Middle-earth as Guardians.
2. Manwë and his wife Elbereth (Varda).
3. The Lady Melian; King Thingol Greycloak of the Sindar.
4. Melkor, later called Morgoth.
5. He stole the Silmarils created by Fëanor.
6. Istari, or Wizards.
7. Valinor, over the Sea.
8. Oromë, the huntsman.
9. By strengthening their goodness and courage.
10. Atop the highest mountain in the world, Oiolossë.

23. More on the Valar

1. d
2. a
3. l
4. n
5. h
6. e
7. k
8. b
9. c
10. i
11. m
12. g
13. f
14. j

PLACES

1. Inns

1. The Ivy Bush
2. The Golden Perch
3. The Prancing Pony
4. The Floating Log
5. The Green Dragon
6. Bridge Inn
7. The Forsaken Inn
8. The Prancing Pony
9. The Prancing Pony
10. The Green Dragon

2. Forests

1. Nimbrethil.
2. A forest of Ents that guarded the Tower of Orthanc to prevent Saruman's escape.
3. Brethil.
4. Fangorn Forest; Fangorn the Ent, oldest surviving Ent.
5. Greenwood the Great.
6. Mirkwood; Eryn Lasgalen.
7. Region.
8. Nan Elmoth.
9. Druadan Forest; Ghân-buri-Ghân and his people, the Wild Men.
10. Old Forest.

3. Moria

1. Khazad-dûm.
2. Sirannon, the Gate-stream.
3. Mellon (friend).
4. Mithril.
5. The Balrog.
6. Orcs, led by Azog.
7. Azog killed Thrór when he returned to Moria. Thrór was an heir of Durin, the Eldest.
8. Balin.
9. Chamber of Mazarbul; the Chamber of Records.
10. The Endless Stair.

4. Mountains and Hills

1. Barazinbar, Zirak-zigil, and Bundushathûr (their Elvish names are Caradhras, Celebdil, and Fanuidhol).
2. Ephel Dúath, and Ered Lithui.
3. Mount Mindolluin.
4. Dwimorberg, the Haunted Mountain.
5. Erebor, the Lonely Mountain.
6. Orodruin, or Mount Doom.
7. Amon Hen; Amon Lhaw.
8. Cerin Amroth.
9. Ered Nimrais, or the White Mountains.
10. Hill of Guard.

5. Rivers

1. Morgulduin.
2. Forest River.
3. Baranduin, or Brandywine.
4. Lefnui, Morthond, Ciril, Ringló, Anduin, Gilrain, Serni.
5. Narog.
6. Anduin.
7. Bruinen.
8. Enchanted River.
9. Sirion.
10. Gelion, Ascar, Thalos, Legolin, Brithlor, Duilwen, Andurant.

6. Towers

1. Amon Dîn, Eilenach, Nardol, Erelas, Min-Rimmon, Calenhad, and Halifiren.
2. Narchost and Carchost.
3. On either side of the great pass Cirith Gorgor.
4. Barad-dûr.
5. The foundations of Barad-dûr could not be destroyed so long as the Ring survived for they were built with the power of the Ring.
6. Elostirion; Elendil.
7. Orthanc.
8. Barad Eithel.
9. Barad Nimras.
10. The Tower of Amon Sûl.

OTHERS

1. Animals

1. Roäc, son of Carc.
2. Crebain, black crows of Fangorn and Dunland.
3. The mearas.
4. Felaróf.
5. Gwaihir, the Windlord.
6. Firebreathing dragons; and cold-drakes.
7. Firebreathing dragon.
8. Oliphaunts, or mûmakil.
9. Wargs.
10. The great werewolf of Angband, slain by Huan.

2. More Animals

1. Ancalagon.
2. Shoot it in the eye.
3. Carcharoth the Wolf.
4. Large, white, horned cattle, often hunted.
5. Shelob the Great.
6. Bard, the Bowman of Esgaroth.
7. Thorondor.
8. Thrushes of Erebor and Dale.
9. The Boar of Everholt.
10. She was the first of the Great Spiders and she wove a web of Unlight around Melkor, allowing him to reach the Trees unseen.

3. Battle Quiz

Battle of Dagorlad	Second Age 3434
Battle of the Gladden Fields	Third Age 2
Battle of the Crossings of Erui	Third Age 1447
Battle of the Camp	Third Age 1944
Battle of Fornost	Third Age 1975
Battle of the Field of Celebrant	Third Age 2510
Battle of Greenfields	Third Age 2747
Battle of the Crossings of Isen	Third Age 2758
Battle of Azanulbizar	Third Age 2799
Battle of the Crossings of Poros	Third Age 2885
Battle of the Five Armies	Third Age 2941
Battle of the Peak	January 23–25, TA 3019
Battle of the Fords of Isen	February 25 and March 2, TA 3019
Battle of the Hornburg	March 3–4, TA 3019
Battle of the Pelennor Fields	March 15, TA 3019
Battle of Dale	March 15–17, TA 3019
Battle of Bywater	November 3, TA 3019

4. More Battles

1. h
2. f
3. a
4. j
5. b
6. i
7. c
8. g
9. e
10. d

5. Emblems

1. c
2. e
3. n
4. j
5. l
6. k
7. f
8. i, sometimes with an S-rune
9. m
10. a
11. g
12. b, or a swan on a white field
13. d
14. h

6. Horses

1. e
2. c
3. f
4. a
5. d
6. b
7. h
8. g
9. Shadowfax
10. Lightfoot

7. Middle-earth Match-up

1. c
2. f
3. i
4. d
5. j
6. a
7. g
8. h
9. b
10. e

8. More Match-ups

1. c
2. f
3. h
4. j
5. a
6. e
7. g
8. i
9. b
10. d

9. Miscellaneous Match-up

1. d
2. g
3. j
4. f
5. a
6. e
7. i
8. h
9. c
10. b

10. The Palantíri

1. Stones used to see, or to talk to, another far away in space or time.
2. Fëanor.
3. Seven.
4. The Palantír of the Tower Hills.
5. The Palantír of Osgiliath.
6. At Emyn Beraid (the Tower Hills), on Amon Sûl (Weathertop), in Annúminas, at Minas Ithil, at Minas Anor, at Orthanc (Isengard), and in Osgiliath.
7. Two aged hands withering in flame; Denethor burned himself while holding the stone.
8. The Palantír of Orthanc.
9. The Ithilstone of Minas Ithil.
10. Elendil.

11. The Riddle Game

1. If Bilbo won Gollum would escort him out of the caverns. If Gollum won he would eat Bilbo.
2. Mountain.
3. Teeth.
4. Wind.
5. Sun on the daisies.
6. Dark.
7. Eggs.
8. Fish.
9. Time.
10. Bilbo asked, "What have I got in my pocket?" The answer was the One Ring.
11. The Valar.

12. The Rings

1. Nine.
2. Three.
3. Under the sky.
4. Vilya, Nenya, and Narya.
5. When the Ring was heated.
6. Sauron, in Orodruin.
7. Each was a band set with a single gem.
8. The rings caused their Dwarven bearers to lust after gold and other precious materials.
9. They were eaten by dragons, along with their bearers.
10. The Nazgûl. Also the Nine Riders or the Black Riders or the Ringwraiths.

13. More on the Rings

1. Celebrimbor, chief of the Elven-smiths; the purpose was to give the ability to make, heal, and preserve.
2. As long as Sauron had the One Ring the Elven bearers never wore their rings.
3. It was an everlasting lengthening of days causing life to be burdensome.
4. Galadriel, Queen of Lórien; and Gandalf the Grey.
5. Isildur of Númenor cut the Ring from Sauron's hand with the broken sword Narsil.
6. Isildur dove into the river Anduin to escape from an Orc-horde and the Ring slipped from his finger.
7. Déagol, a Stoor Hobbit, and his murderer, Sméagol (Gollum), also a Stoor Hobbit.
8. They became invisible.
9. The Nine were destroyed, the others became powerless.
10. In Elvish runes. In the Black Speech.

14. Weapons

1. They shone with a blue light in the presence of Orcs.
2. Biter and Beater.
3. c
4. e
5. h
6. a
7. j
8. g
9. b
10. i
11. d
12. f
13. Andúril.
14. Flame of the West (also Sword that was Broken).

15. Trees

1. Galathilion.
2. Mallorn.
3. Telperion and Laurelin.
4. They brought Light to Valinor.
5. Lebethron.
6. It was a dead White Tree of Gondor which stood in the Court of Fountain from Third Age 2852 to 3019, until a sapling to replace it could be found.
7. Nimloth.
8. Morgoth (Melkor the Vala).
9. The Party Tree.
10. Hírilorn.

16. Who killed _____ ?

1. Gandalf the Grey.
2. Éowyn and Meriadoc Brandybuck.
3. Bard the Bowman, of Esgaroth.
4. Dáin II.
5. Beorn.
6. The Balrog of Khazad-dûm.
7. Éomer, Third Marshal of Rohan.
8. Gríma Wormtongue.
9. Melkor, or Morgoth.
10. Gothmog, Lord of the Balrogs.